Alfred Edersheim

Israel in Canaan under Joshua and the Judges by Rev. Dr. Edersheim

Alfred Edersheim

Israel in Canaan under Joshua and the Judges by Rev. Dr. Edersheim

ISBN/EAN: 9783743358577

Manufactured in Europe, USA, Canada, Australia, Japa

Cover: Foto ©Lupo / pixelio.de

Manufactured and distributed by brebook publishing software (www.brebook.com)

Alfred Edersheim

Israel in Canaan under Joshua and the Judges by Rev. Dr. Edersheim

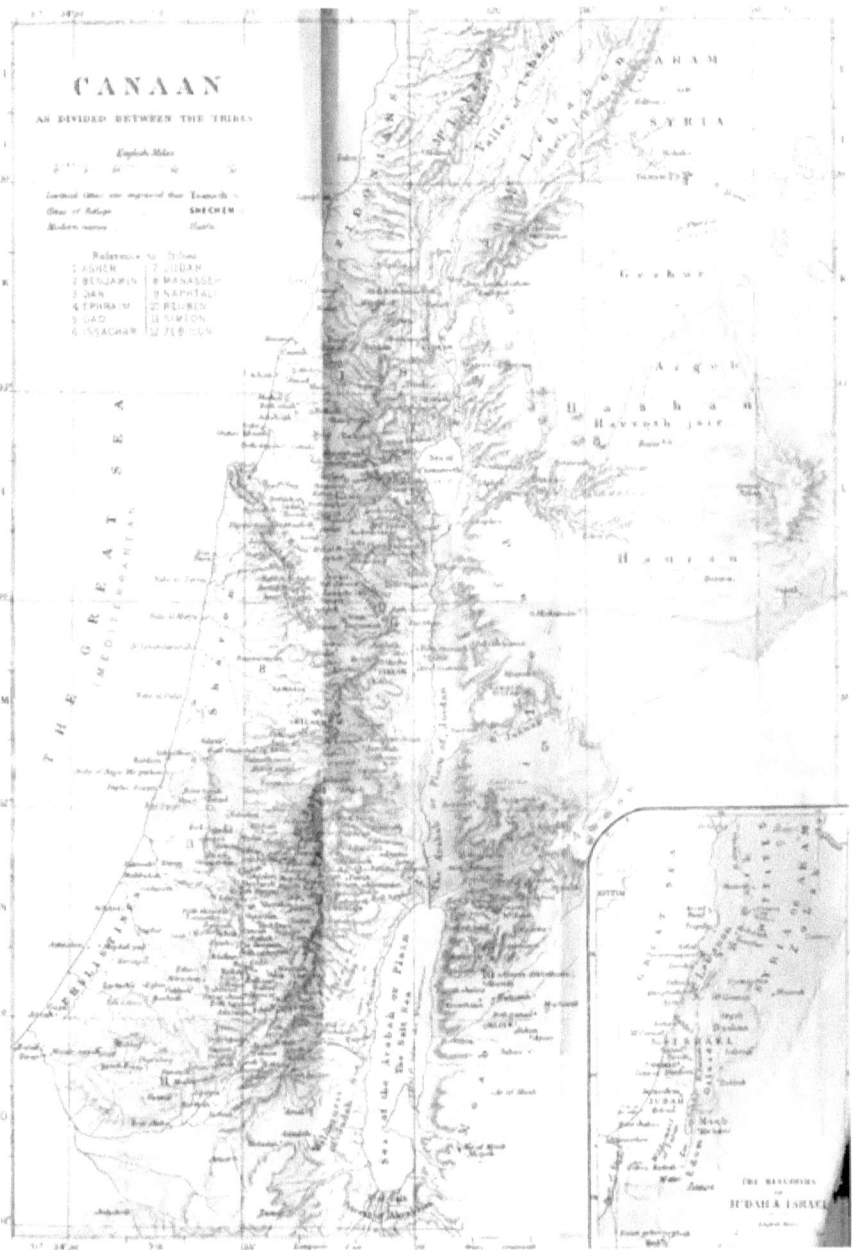

UNDER

JOSHUA AND THE JUDGES.

BY THE

REV. DR. EDERSHEIM,

AUTHOR OF

"THE TEMPLE, ITS MINISTRY AND SERVICES," "THE BIBLE HISTORY," ETC.

LONDON

THE RELIGIOUS TRACT SOCIETY

4 BOUVERIE STREET AND 65 ST. PAUL'S CHURCHYARD, E.C.

PRINTED BY WILLIAM CLOWES AND SONS, LIMITED,
DUKE STREET, STAMFORD STREET, S.E., AND GREAT WINDMILL STREET, W.

PREFACE.

THE history of Israel as a nation may be said to commence with their entrance into their own land. All previous to this—from the Paschal night on which Israel was born as a people to the overthrow of Sihon and of Og, the last who would have barred Israel's way to their home—had been only preparatory. During the forty years' wanderings the people had, so to speak, been welded together by the strong hand of Jehovah. But now, when the Lion of Judah couched by the banks of Jordon, Israel was face to face with its grand mission, and the grand task of its national life commenced : to dispossess heathenism, and to plant in its stead the Kingdom of God (Ps. lxxx. 8-11), which was destined to strike root and to grow, till, in the fulness of time, it would extend to all nations of the world.[1]

Accordingly, when the camp of Israel was pitched at Shittim, a new period commenced. Its history records, first, certain events which had to take place immediately before entering the Land of Promise ; next, the conquest, and then the apportionment of the land among the tribes of Israel ; and, lastly, in the time of the Judges, side by side, the unfolding of Israel's religious and national condition, and the assertion of those fundamental principles which underlay its very existence as a God-called people. These principles are :—The special relationship of Israel as the people of God towards Jehovah, and Jehovah's special dealings towards them as

---

[1] Comp. such a Missionary Psalm as the 87th ; also such passages as Ps. lxxxvi. 9 ; Is. xliv. 5.

their King.[1] The history of the wilderness period had, indeed, been shaped by this two-fold relationship, but its consequences appeared more clearly under Joshua, and most fully in the time of the Judges. When not only Moses, but Joshua, and even the elders who had been his contemporaries had passed away, the people, now settled in the land, were left free to develop those tendencies which had all along existed. Then ensued that alternation of national apostacy and judgment, and of penitent return to God and deliverance, which constitutes, so to speak, the framework on which the Book of Judges is constructed. This part of Israel's history attained alike its highest and its lowest point in Samson, with whom the period of the Judges appropriately closes. For, the administration of Samuel forms only the transition to, and preparation for the establishment of royalty in Israel. But the spiritual import of the whole history of that period is summed up in these words of Holy Scripture (Ps. xliv. 2-4) : "Thou didst drive out the heathen with Thy hand, and plantedst them : Thou didst afflict the people, and cast them out. For they got not the land in possession by their own sword, neither did their own arm save them, but Thy right hand, and Thine arm, and the light of Thy countenance, because thou hadst a favour unto them. Thou art my King, O God : command deliverances for Jacob."

The Books of Joshua and of the Judges form the two first portions of what in the Hebrew Canon are designated as the "Former Prophets."[2] This, not because their narratives are largely connected with the rise and activity of the prophets, nor yet because their authors were prophets, but rather because the character and contents of these books are prophetic. They give the history of Israel from the prophet's point of view—not a succinct and successive chronicle of the nation, but a history of the Kingdom of God in Israel. This also explains its peculiarities of form and style. For, neither are the Judges, for example, mentioned in the order

---

[1] Some modern negative critics have even broached the theory—of course, wholly unfounded—that originally the Book of Joshua had formed with the five books of Moses a *Hexateuch*.

[2] The others are the Books of Samuel and of the Kings.

of their succession, nor must it be supposed that they ruled over all the tribes of Israel. Similarly, there are evidently large blanks left in the history of the times, and while some events or reigns of considerable duration are only cursorily mentioned, very detailed and circumstantial narratives are given of persons and occurrences, which only occupied the scene for a comparatively short period. But as, from the frequent references to authorities, and from their evident knowledge of details, the writers of these books must have had at command ample material for a full history, we conclude that the selection, Divinely guided, was made in accordance with the "Spirit of Prophecy," to mark the progress of the Kingdom of God in connection with Israel.

From what has been said it will be readily understood, that the history traced in this volume offers peculiar difficulties—from its briefness, its abruptness, its rapid transitions, the unusual character of its incidents, and its sudden and marked Divine interpositions. These difficulties are not so much exegetical or critical—although such are certainly not wanting—but rather concern the substance of the narratives themselves, and touch the very essence of Holy Scripture. For myself, I am free to confess that I entered on my present undertaking, I shall not say with apprehension, but with great personal diffidence. I knew, indeed, that what appears a difficulty might find its full and satisfactory solution, even though I were not able to indicate it, and that a narrative might have its Divine meaning and spiritual purpose, even though I should fail to point it out. Yet I imagine that most readers of the Books of Joshua and Judges will in some measure understand and sympathise with my feelings. All the more is it now alike duty and privilege, at the close of these investigations, to express it joyously and thankfully, that the more fully these narratives are studied, the more luminous will they become; the more will their Divine meaning appear; and the more will they carry to the mind conviction of their truthfulness, and to the heart lessons of their spiritual import. Perhaps I may be allowed in illustration of these statements to point to my study of the characters of Balaam and Joshua, and of the histories of Gideon, of Jephthah, and especially of Samson.

From this circumstance, and faithful to the plan, which I proposed to myself in this series, of gradually leading a reader onwards, the sacred narrative has received in this volume more full treatment—the discussion of such textual questions as fell within its scope, being, however, chiefly thrown into the *foot-notes*. Many questions, indeed, on which I could have earnestly wished to enter, lay quite outside the purport of the present series, and had therefore reluctantly to be left aside. These concern chiefly the *antiquity* and the *authenticity* of these books of Holy Scripture. I venture to think, that a great deal yet remains to be said on these points—the chief defect of former treatises lying, in my opinion, in this, that they rather busy themselves with refuting the arguments of opponents, than bring forward what I would call the *positive* evidence. That such positive evidence abundantly exists, a somewhat careful study has increasingly convinced me. I am not ashamed to own my belief that, notwithstanding confident assertions of writers on the opposite side, we may trustfully and contentedly walk in "the old paths;" and the present volume is intended as a reverent contribution, however inadequate, towards the better understanding of what, I verily believe, "holy men of old spake as they were moved by the Spirit," and that, "for doctrine, for reproof, for correction, for instruction in righteousness."

ALFRED EDERSHEIM.

LODERS VICARAGE, BRIDPORT.
February 23, 1877.

CONTENTS.

CHAPTER I.

ISRAEL ABOUT TO TAKE POSSESSION OF THE LAND OF PROMISE—DECISIVE CONTEST SHOWING THE REAL CHARACTER OF HEATHENISM—CHARACTER AND HISTORY OF BALAAM . 11

CHAPTER II.

THE "PROPHECIES" OF BALAAM — THE END OF BALAAM — PARALLEL BETWEEN BALAAM AND JUDAS 23

CHAPTER III.

THE SECOND CENSUS OF ISRAEL — THE "DAUGHTERS OF ZELOPHEHAD"—APPOINTMENT OF MOSES' SUCCESSOR—SACRIFICIAL ORDINANCES—THE WAR AGAINST MIDIAN—ALLOCATION OF TERRITORY EAST OF THE JORDAN—LEVITICAL AND CITIES OF REFUGE 33

CHAPTER IV.

DEATH AND BURIAL OF MOSES 42

CHAPTER V.

THE CHARGE TO JOSHUA—DESPATCH OF THE TWO SPIES TO JERICHO—RAHAB 46

CHAPTER VI.

THE MIRACULOUS PARTING OF JORDAN, AND THE PASSAGE OF THE CHILDREN OF ISRAEL—GILGAL AND ITS MEANING—THE FIRST PASSOVER ON THE SOIL OF PALESTINE . . 53

CHAPTER VII.

The "Prince of the Host of Jehovah" appears to Joshua—The Miraculous Fall of Jericho before the Ark of Jehovah 58

CHAPTER VIII.

Unsuccessful Attack upon Ai—Achan's Sin, and Judgment—Ai Attacked a second time and taken . . 63

CHAPTER IX.

Solemn Dedication of the Land and of Israel on Mounts Ebal and Gerizim—The Deceit of the Gibeonites . 72

CHAPTER X.

The Battle of Gibeon—Conquest of the South of Canaan—The Battle of Merom—Conquest of the North of Canaan—State of the Land at the close of the Seven Years' War 80

CHAPTER XI.

Distribution of the Land—Unconquered Districts—Tribes east of the Jordan—"The Lot"—Tribes west of the Jordan—The Inheritance of Caleb—Dissatisfaction of the Sons of Joseph—The Tabernacle at Shiloh—Final Division of the Land 87

CHAPTER XII.

Return of the two and a half Tribes to their Homes—Building of an Altar by them—Embassy to them—Joshua's Farewell Addresses—Death of Joshua—Review of his Life and Work. 96

CHAPTER XIII.

Summary of the Book of Judges—Judah's and Simeon's Campaign—Spiritual and National Decay of Israel—"From Gilgal to Bochim." 105

CHAPTER XIV.

Othniel—Ehud—Shamgar. 114

CHAPTER XV.

The Oppression of Jabin and Sisera—Deborah and Barak—The Battle of Taanach—The Song of Deborah . 119

CHAPTER XVI.

Midianitish Oppression—The Calling of Gideon—Judgment begins at the House of God—The Holy War—The Night-battle of Moreh 130

CHAPTER XVII.

Farther Course of Gideon—The Ephod at Ophrah—Death of Gideon—Conspiracy of Abimelech—The Parable of Jotham—Rule and End of Abimelech . 142

CHAPTER XVIII.

Successors of Abimelech—Chronology of the Period—Israel's renewed Apostasy, and their humiliation before Jehovah—Oppression by the Ammonites—Jephthah—His History and Vow—The Successors of Jephthah 152

CHAPTER XIX.

Meaning of the History of Samson—His Annunciation and Early History—The Spirit of Jehovah "impels him"—His Deeds of Faith 163

CHAPTER XX.

The Sin and Fall of Samson—Jehovah departs from him—Samson's Repentance, Faith, and Death . . . 173

CHAPTER XXI.

Social and Religious Life in Bethlehem in the days of the Judges—The Story of Ruth—King David's Ancestors 177

CHRONOLOGICAL TABLE,

ACCORDING TO PROFESSOR KEIL, FROM THE EXODUS TO THE BUILDING OF THE TEMPLE BY SOLOMON.

(Comp. Judges xi. 26 and 1 Kings vi. 1.)

PRINCIPAL EVENTS.	Years of their duration.	Date before Christ.
The Exodus	..	.. 1492
Giving of the Law on Mount Sinai	..	from 1492 to 1491
Death of Moses and Aaron	in the 40th year	.. 1453
Conquest of Canaan by Joshua	7	1452 ,, 1445
Division of Canaan to the invasion of Chushan Rishathaim	10	1445 ,, 1435
Death of Joshua	..	about 1442
Wars of Israel against the Canaanites	..	from 1442
Expedition against Benjamin (Judges xx.)	..	about 1436
Oppression by Chushan Rishathaim	8	1435 to 1427
Othniel, and rest of Israel	40	1427 ,, 1387
Oppression by the Moabites	18	1387 ,, 1369
Ehud, and rest of Israel	80	1369 ,, 1289
Victory of Shamgar over the Philistines	..	.. ..
Oppression by Jabin	20	1289 ,, 1269
Deborah and Barak, and rest of Israel	40	1269 ,, 1229
Oppression by the Midianites	7	1229 ,, 1222
Gideon, and rest	40	1222 ,, 1182
Abimelech	3	1182 ,, 1179
Tola	23	1179 ,, 1156
Jair	22	1156 ,, 1134
Eli for forty years	..	1154 ,, 1114
Then: *In the East.* *In the West.*		
Oppression by the Ammonites, 18 years: 1134-1116 — By the Philistines	40	1134 ,, 1094
Loss of the Ark	..	about 1114
Jephthah, 6 years: 1116-1110 — Samson's deeds	..	1116 to 1096
Samuel as a prophet	..	from 1114
Ibzan, 7 years: 1110-1103 — Samuel judge	19	1094 to 1075
Elon, 10 years: 1103-1093 — Saul king	20	1075 ,, 1055
Abdon, 8 years: 1093-1085 — David at Hebron	7	1055 ,, 1048
David at Jerusalem	33	1048 ,, 1015
Solomon to the building of Temple	3	1015 ,, 1012
Total	480 years.	

Israel in Canaan,

UNDER

Joshua and the Judges.

CHAPTER I.

Israel about to take Possession of the Land of Promise—Decisive Contest showing the real Character of Heathenism—Character and History of Balaam.

(Numb. xxii.)

THE wilderness-life and the early contests of Israel were over. Israel stood on the threshold of the promised possession, separated from it only by the waters of Jordan. But, before crossing that boundary-line, it was absolutely necessary that the people should, once and for all, gain full knowledge of the real character of heathenism in its relation to the kingdom of God. Israel must learn that the heathen nations were not only hostile *political* powers, opposing their progress, but that heathenism itself was in its nature antagonistic to the kingdom of God. The two were incompatible, and therefore no alliance could ever be formed with heathenism, no intercourse cultivated, nor even its presence tolerated. This was the lesson which, on the eve of entering Palestine, Israel was to learn by painful experience in connection with the history of Balaam. Its importance at that particular period will readily be understood. Again and again was the same lesson taught throughout the history of Israel, as each alliance or even contact with the kingdoms of this world brought fresh sorrow and trouble. Nor is its application to the Church of God, so far as concerns the danger of com mixture with, and conformity to the world, less obvious. And so the history of Balak and of Balaam has, besides its direct lessons, a deep meaning for all times.

With the decisive victories over Sihon and over Og, all who could have barred access to the Land of Promise had been either left behind, or else scattered and defeated. And now the camp of Israel had moved forward, in the language of Scripture, to "the other side Jordan from Jericho."[1] Their tents were pitched in rich meadow-land, watered by many streams, which rush down from the neighbouring mountains— the *Arboth*, or lowlands of *Moab*, as the country on this and that side the river was still called, after its more ancient inhabitants.[2] As the vast camp lay scattered over a width of several miles, from *Abel Shittim*, "the meadow of the acacias," in the north, to *Beth Jeshimoth*, "the house of desolations," on the edge of the desert, close to the Dead Sea, in the south,[3] it might have seemed as if the lion of Judah were couching ready for his spring on the prey. But was he the lion of Judah, and were the promises of God to him indeed "yea and amen?" A fiercer assault, and one in which heathenism would wield other arms than those which had so lately been broken in their hands, would soon decide that question.

We can perceive many reasons why Moab, though apparently not immediately threatened, should, at that special moment, have come forward as the champion and representative of heathenism.[4] True, Israel had left their land untouched, restrained by express Divine command from invading it.[5] But their close neighbourhood was dangerous. Besides, had not all that land north of the Arnon, which Israel had just wrested from

---

[1] Or, "across the Jordan of Jericho," *i.e.*, that part of the Jordan which watered Jericho.
[2] The name *Arboth* still survives in the *Arabah*, which stretches from a little farther south to the Elanitic Gulf of the Red Sea.
[3] Numb. xxxiii. 49.   [4] Numb. xxii. 1-3.   [5] Deut. ii. 9.

the Amorites, been till lately Moabitish—the very name of Moab still lingering on mountain-plateau and lowland plains; and might not Moab again have what once it held? But there was far more involved than either fear or cupidity suggested. The existence alike of heathen nations and of heathenism itself depended on the issue. There can be no doubt that the prophetic anticipation of the song of Moses [1] had already in great part been fulfilled. "The nations" *had* "heard" of God's marvellous doings for Israel, and were afraid; "the mighty men of Moab, trembling" *had* taken "hold upon them." Among the wandering tribes of the east, tidings, especially of this kind, travel fast. Jethro had heard them long before,[2] and the testimony of Rahab[3] shows how fear and dread had fallen upon the inhabitants of the land. Force of arms had been tried against them. The Amorites, who had been able to wrest from Moab all the land north of the Arnon, had boldly marched against Israel under the leadership of Sihon their king, and been not only defeated but almost exterminated. A similar fate had befallen the brave king of Bashan and his people. There could be no question that so far Jehovah, the God of Israel, had proved true to His word, and stronger than the gods of the nations who had been subdued. Farther progress, then, in the same direction might prove fatal alike to their national existence, their national deities, and their national religion.

In trying to realise the views and feelings of heathenism under such circumstances, we must beware of transporting into them our modern ideas. In our days the question is as to the acknowledgment or else the denial of Jehovah God. In those days it turned upon the acknowledgment or the opposite of Jehovah as the *only* true and living God, as this is expressed in the first commandment. Heathenism would never have thought of denying the existence or power of Jehovah as the national God of the Hebrews (see, for example, 1 Kings xx. 23; 2 Kings xviii. 25, 33-35). What it controverted was, that Jehovah was the *only* God—all others being merely idols,

---

[1] Ex. xv. 14-16.   [2] Ex. xviii. 1.   [3] Josh. ii. 9.

the work of men's hands. Prepared as they were to acknowledge Jehovah as the national Deity of the Hebrews, the question before them would be, whether *He* or their gods were the more powerful. It was a point of the deepest interest to them, since, if anything were known of Jehovah, it would be this that He was "a jealous God," and that the rites by which He was worshipped were so different from theirs, as to involve an entire change, not only of religion, but of popular habits and manners. From what has been stated, it will be understood why, in attempting to break the power of Israel, whose God had hitherto—whether from accident, fate, or inherent power—proved Himself superior to those of the nations, the king of Moab had, in the first place, recourse to "divination," and why he was so specially anxious to secure the services of Balaam.

Balaam, or rather Bileam, the son of Beor,[1] belonged apparently to a family of magicians who resided at Pethor, possibly, as has been suggested, a city of professional soothsayers or students of that craft, but certainly situated in "Aram" or Mesopotamia, and on the banks of the Euphrates.[2] His name, which means "devourer," or "swallower up," and that of his father, which means "burner up," or "destroyer"—whether given them at birth, or, as is so common in the East, from their supposed characteristics—indicate alike the claims which they put forth and the estimate in which they were popularly held.[3] If, as has been conjectured,[4] Balak, the king of Moab, was of Midianitish origin (his father having been a Midianitish usurper), it becomes all the more intelligible that in his peculiar circumstances he would apply for advice and help to the Midianites;

---

[1] By a peculiar Aramaic interchange of letters, St. Peter writes the name *Bosor:* 2 Pet. ii. 15.

[2] Numb. xxii. 5; xxiii. 7; Deut. xxiii. 4.

[3] It is of curious interest, that precisely the same names occur in the royal Edomitish family: Gen. xxxvi. 32.

[4] By Bishop Harold Browne, from the analogy of his father's name to that of later Midianite chiefs—the name *Zippor,* "bird," reminding us of *Oreb,* "crow," and *Zeeb,* "wolf." The later Targumim also regard Balak as of Midianitish origin.

that he would ally himself with them; and that through them he would come to know of, and along with them send for, Balaam.[1] At any rate, those Midianite wanderers of the desert which stretched between Mesopotamia and the dominions of Moab would, like modern Bedawîn under similar circumstances, not only know of the existence of a celebrated magician like Balaam, but probably greatly exaggerate his power. Moreover, being themselves unable to attack Israel, they would nevertheless gladly make common cause with Moab, and that, although for the present their territory was not directly threatened, any more than that of the Moabites. This explains the alliance of Moab and Midian and their common embassy to Balaam.

The object in view was twofold. As already explained, the success of Israel as against the nations, or rather that of Israel's God against their deities, might, in their opinion, arise from one of two causes. Either their own national deities—Chemosh and Baal—had not been sufficiently propitiated—sufficient influence or power had not been brought to bear upon them; or else Jehovah was *really* stronger than they. In either case Balaam would bring invaluable, and, if he only chose to exert it, *sure* help. For, according to heathen views, a magician had absolute and irresistible power with the gods; power was inherent in him or in the incantations which he used. And herein lay one of the fundamental differences between heathenism and the Old Testament, between magic and miracles. In the former it was all of man, in the latter it was shown to be all of God. No prophet of the Lord ever had or claimed power, like the magicians; but in every case the gracious influence was specially, and for that time, transmitted directly from God. Only the God-Man had power in Himself, so that His every contact brought health and life. And in the Christian dispensation also, however much of the supernatural there may be experienced and witnessed, nothing is magical; there is no mere exercise of power or of authority;

[1] Numb. xxii. 4, 7, etc.

but all is conveyed to us through the free promises of God, and in the dispensation of His grace.

But to return. Supposing that Jehovah were really superior to Chemosh and Baal, the king of Moab and his associates would none the less desire the aid of Balaam. For it was a further principle of heathenism, that national deities might be induced to transfer their blessing and protection from one nation to another. Thus the ancient Romans were wont, when laying siege to a foreign city, solemnly to invite its special gods to come out to them and join their side,[1] promising them in return not only equal but higher honours than they had hitherto enjoyed. And if something of this kind were now needful—if influence was to be exerted on the God of the Israelites, who was so capable of it as Balaam, both from his profession as a dealer with the gods, and from his special qualifications? And this leads up to the principal personage in this history, to his character, and to the question of his religion.[2]

What has been said of the knowledge which the king of Moab must have possessed of Jehovah's dealings in reference to Israel[3] applies, of course, with much greater force to Balaam himself. As a professional magician, belonging to a family of magicians, and residing at one of their chief seats, it was alike

---

[1] See the proof passages in Kurtz' *History of the Old Covenant*, vol. iii. p. 399; and the very interesting discussion on the subject by Döllinger, in his splendid work, *Heidenthum u. Judenthum*.

[2] As this is not the place for theological or critical discussion, I will only remark, that I cannot accept either of the opposing views of Balaam's character—that he was a true prophet of Jehovah, or that he was simply "a prophet of the devil," "who was *compelled* by God, against his will, to bless." But as little do I profess myself able to receive, or even properly to understand, the view of recent critics (Hengsterberg, Kurtz, Keil, Bishop Harold Browne, etc.), that Balaam "was in a transition state from one to the other," that "he knew and confessed Jehovah, sought and found him;" but that, "on the other hand, he was not sufficiently advanced in the knowledge and service of Jehovah to throw overboard every kind of heathen augury." I have, therefore, subjected the whole question to fresh investigation, the results of which are given in the text.

[3] Ex. xv. 14-16.

his duty and his interest to acquaint himself with such matters. Moreover, we ought not to forget that, in the place of his residence, traditions of Abraham would linger with that Eastern local tenacity which we have already had so frequent occasion to notice. Indeed, we have positive evidence that Balaam's inquiries had gone back far beyond the recent dealings of Jehovah to His original covenant-relationship towards His people. A comparison of the promise of God to Abraham in Gen. xiii. 16 with the mode of expression used by Balaam in Numb. xxiii. 10; still more—the correspondence between Gen. xlix. 9 and Numb. xxiii. 24, xxiv. 9 in his description of Judah; but most of all, the virtual repetition of the prophecy Gen. xlix. 10 in Numb. xxiv. 17, prove beyond doubt that Balaam had made himself fully acquainted with the promises of Jehovah to Israel. That a professional soothsayer like Balaam should have been quite ready, upon a review of their whole history, to acknowledge Jehovah as the national God of Israel, and to enter—if the expression may be allowed—into professional relationship with such a powerful Deity, seems only natural in the circumstances. This explains *his* conduct in speaking to and of Jehovah, and apparently owning Him. *But in all this Balaam did not advance a step beyond the mere heathen point of view*, any more than Simon Magus when, "beholding the miracles and signs which were done," "he was baptised;"[1] nor did his conduct bring him nearer to the true service of Jehovah than were those seven sons of Sceva to that of Christ, when they endeavoured to cast out evil spirits in the name of the Lord Jesus.[2] In fact, Scripture designates him uniformly by the word *Kosem*, which is the distinctive term for heathen soothsayers in opposition to prophets of the Lord. And with this his whole conduct agrees. Had he possessed even the most elementary knowledge of Jehovah as *the only true and living God*, or the most rudimentary understanding of His covenant-purposes, he could not, *considering his acquaintance with previous prophecy*, have for a moment entertained the idea of allying himself with

[1] Acts viii. 13.   [2] Acts xix. 13, 14.

Balak against Israel. On the other hand, if, according to his view of the matter, he could have succeeded in making the God of Israel, so to speak, one of his patron-deities, and if, upon his own terms, he could have become one of His prophets; still more, if he could have gained such influence with Him as to turn Him from His purpose regarding Israel, then would he have reached the goal of his ambition, and become by far the most powerful magician in the world. Thus, in our opinion, from the time when we first meet him, standing where the two roads part, to the bitter end of his treachery, when, receiving the reward of Judas, he was swept away in the destruction of Midian, his conduct was throughout consistently *heathen*, and his progress rapid in the downward course.

Where the two roads part! In every great crisis of history, and, we feel persuaded, in the great crisis of every individual life, there is such a meeting and parting of the two ways—to life or to destruction. It was so in the case of Pharaoh, when Moses first brought him the summons of the Lord to let His people go free, proving his authority by indubitable signs. And Balaam stood at the meeting and parting of the two ways that night when the ambassadors of Balak and the elders of Midian were for the first time under his roof. *That embassy was the crisis in his history.* He had advanced to the knowledge that Jehovah, the God of Israel, was God. The question now came: Would he recognise Him as the only true and living God, with Whom no such relationship could exist as those which heathenism supposed; towards Whom every relationship must be moral and spiritual, not magical—one of heart and of life service, not of influence and power? To use New Testament language, in his general acknowledgment of Jehovah, Balaam had advanced to the position described in the words: "he that is not against us is for us."[1] But this is only, as it were, the meeting and parting of the two roads. The next question which comes is far deeper, and decisive, so far as each individual is concerned. It

---

[1] Luke ix. 50.

refers to our relationship to the Person of Christ. And in regard to this we read: "He that is not with Me is against Me."[1]

As always in such circumstances, God's great mercy and infinite patience and condescension were not wanting to help Balaam in the crisis of his life. There could, at least, be no doubt on two points. Balak's avowed wish had been, by the help of Balaam, to "smite" Israel and "drive them out of the land;"[2] and his expressed conviction, "he whom thou blessest is blessed, and he whom thou cursest is cursed." Now, not to speak of the implied magical power thus attributed to him, Balaam must have known that Balak's intention ran directly counter to Jehovah's purpose, while the words, in which the power of blessing and cursing was ascribed to Balaam, were not only a transference to man of what belonged to God alone, *but must have been known to Balaam* as the very words in which Jehovah had originally bestowed the blessing on Abraham: "I will bless them that bless thee, and curse him that curseth thee."[3] That Balaam so knew these words appears from his own quotation of them in Numb. xxiv. 9. The proposal of Balak therefore ran directly counter to the fundamental purpose of God, as Balaam knew it—and yet he could hesitate even for a single moment! But this is not all. In His infinite long-suffering, not willing that any should perish, God even now condescended to Balaam. He had proposed to the ambassadors of Balak that they should "lodge" with him that night, and that on the morrow he would make his reply, as Jehovah would speak unto him. And Jehovah did condescend to meet Balaam in his own way, and that night fully communicated to him His will. The garbled and misrepresenting account of it, which Balaam in the morning gave to his guests, finally marked his choice and decided his fate.

But why did Jehovah God appear to, or deal with such an one as Balaam? Questions like these ought, with our limited knowledge of God's purposes, not always to be entertained. In the present instance, however, we can suggest at least some

[1] Matt. xii. 30.   [2] Numb. xxii. 6.   [3] Gen. xii. 3.

answer. Of God's purpose, so far as Balaam's personal condition was concerned, we have already spoken. But a wider issue was here to be tried. Balak had sent for Balaam in order through his magic to destroy Israel, or rather to arrest and turn aside the wonder-working power of Jehovah. It was, therefore, really a contest between heathenism and Israel as the people of God, which would exhibit and decide the real relationship between Israel and the heathen world, or in other words, between the Church of God and the kingdoms of this world. And as formerly God had raised up Pharaoh to be the instrument of bringing down the gods of Egypt, so would He now decide this contest through the very man whom Balak had chosen as its champion—using him as a willing instrument, if he yielded, or as an unwilling, if he rebelled, but in any case as an *efficient* instrument for carrying out His own purposes. It is in this manner that we regard God's meeting Balaam, and His speaking both to him and through him.

Three brief but emphatic utterances had God in that first night made to Balaam: " Thou shalt not go with them; thou shalt not curse the people: for they are blessed."[1] Of these Balaam, in his reply to the ambassadors next morning, had deliberately suppressed the last two (xxii. 13). Yet they were the most important, as showing the utter hopelessness of the undertaking, and the utter powerlessness of any man to control or influence the purpose of God. He thus withheld knowledge of the utmost importance for understanding alike the character of the true God and that of His true servants, who simply obey, but do not seek to control, His will. But even in what he did repeat of God's message there was grievous misrepresentation. For this statement, "Jehovah refuses to give me leave to go with you" (xxii. 13), implied an ungrounded arbitrariness on the part of God; confirmed Balak in his heathen views; and perhaps encouraged him to hope for better results under more favourable circumstances. As for Balaam himself, we may be allowed to infer, that he misunderstood God's appearance to, and conversa-

[1] Numb. xxii. 12.

tion with him, as implying a sort of league with, or acknowledgment of him, while all the time he had irrevocably departed from God, and entered the way of sin and of judgment. Accordingly, we find Balaam thenceforth speaking of Jehovah as " my God," and confidently assuming the character of His servant. At the same time, he secured for himself the presents of Balak, while, in his reply, he took care not to lose the favour of the king, but rather to make him all the more anxious to gain his aid, since he *was* owned of Jehovah, Who had only refused a leave which on another occasion He might grant.

It was under these circumstances that a second embassy from Balak and Midian, more honourable than the first, and with almost unlimited promises, came again to ask Balaam " to curse this people" (ver. 17). The king had well judged. With no spiritual, only a heathen acknowledgment of Jehovah, covetousness and ambition were the main actuating motives of Balaam. In the pithy language of the New Testament,[1] he "loved the wages of unrighteousness." But already his course was sealed. Refusing to yield himself a willing, he would now be made the unwilling instrument of exalting Jehovah. And thus God gave him leave to do that on which he had set his heart, with this important reservation, however: " But yet the word which I shall say unto thee, that shalt thou do." Balaam, whose blinded self-satisfaction had already appeared in his profession to the ambassadors, that he could "not go beyond the word of Jehovah his God," understood not the terrible judgment upon himself implied in this " let him alone," which gave up the false prophet to his own lusts. He had no doubt been so far honest, although he was grossly and wilfully ignorant of all that concerned Jehovah, when he proposed to consult God a second time, whether he might curse Israel. And now it seemed as if God had indeed inclined to him. Balaam was as near reaching the ideal of a magician, and having " power," as was Simon Magus when he offered the apostles money to bestow on him the power of imparting the Holy Ghost.

[1] 2 Pet. ii. 15.

It was no doubt on account of this spirit of deluded self-satisfaction, in which next morning he accompanied the ambassadors of Balak, that "God's anger was kindled because he went,"[1] and that "the angel of Jehovah stood in the way for an adversary against him"—significantly, the angel of the covenant with a drawn sword, threatening destruction. The main object of what happened to him on the journey was, if possible, to arouse Balaam to a sense of his utter ignorance of, and alienation from Jehovah. And so even "the dumb ass, speaking with man's voice, forbad the madness of the prophet."[2] We know, indeed, that animals are often more sensitive to the presence or nearness of danger than man—as it were, perceive what escapes our senses. But in this case the humiliating lesson was, that while the self-satisfied prophet had absolutely seen nothing, his ass had perceived the presence of the angel, and, by going out of the way, or falling down, saved the life of his master; and that, even so, Balaam still continued blinded, perverse, and misunderstanding, till God opened the mouth of the dumb animal, so that with man's voice it might forbid the madness of the prophet. To show Balaam himself as he really was, and the consequences of his conduct; and to do so in the strongest, that is, in this case, in the most humiliating manner, such was the object of the apparition of the angel, and of the human language in which Balaam heard the ass reproving him.[3]

But even this produced no real effect—only an offer on the part of Balaam to get him back again, if it displeased the angel of Jehovah (xxii. 34). The proposal was as blundering, and argued as deep ignorance, as his former readiness to go with the ambassadors. For the question was not simply one of

[1] Literally, "because he was going." Keil rightly points out that the use of the participle here implies, that God's anger was kindled by the spirit and disposition in which he was going, rather than by the fact of his going.

[2] 2 Pet. ii. 16.

[3] This is not the place to enter into critical discussions. The great matter is to understand the meaning and object of this narrative, in whatever manner the "man's voice" may have issued from the "dumb ass," or the human language have reached the consciousness of Balaam.

going or not going, but of glorifying God, and acknowledging the supremacy of His covenant-purpose. Balaam might have gone and returned without doing this; but Jehovah would now do it Himself through Balaam. And already the elders of Moab and Midian had hurried on along with Balaam's own servants, to announce the arrival of the prophet. Presently from the lonely, terrible interview with the angel was he to pass into the presence of the representative of that heathenism against which the drawn sword in the angel's hand was really stretched out.

CHAPTER II.

The "Prophecies" of Balaam—The End of Balaam—Parallel between Balaam and Judas.

(NUMB. XXII. 36–XXV.; XXXI. 1–20.)

THE meeting between the king of Moab and the soothsayer took place at Ir Moab, the "city" or capital of Moab, close by its northern boundary.[1] It commenced with gentle reproaches on the part of the monarch, which, Eastern-like, covered large promises, to which the soothsayer replied by repeating his old profession of being only able to speak the word that God would put in his mouth. There is no need of assuming hypocrisy on his part; both monarch and soothsayer acted quite in character and quite consistently. From Ir Moab they proceeded to Kirjath Huzoth, "the city of streets," the later Kiriathaim.[2] Here, or in the immediate neighbourhood, the first sacrifices were offered, Balaam as well as "the princes" taking part in the sacrificial meal. Next morning

---

[1] Canon Tristram identifies this with the old *Ar*, or *Rabbath Moab* (*Land of Moab*, p. 110). But this latter seems too far south for the requirements of the text.

[2] Josh. xiii. 19; Ezek. xxv. 9, etc. See the description of the place, and of the prospect from it, in Tristram, *u.s.*, pp. 270, 276.

Balak took the soothsayer to the lofty heights of Mount Attarus, to *Bamoth Baal*, "the heights of Baal," so-called because that plateau was dedicated to the service of Baal. The spot, which also bears the names of Baal-meon, Beth Baal-meon, and Beth-meon, commands a magnificent view. Although "too far recessed to show the depression of the Dead Sea," the view northwards stretches as far as Jerusalem, Gerizim, Tabor, Hermon, and Mount Gilead.[1] But, although the eye could sweep so far over the Land of Promise, he would, from the conformation of the mountains, only see "the utmost part of the people,"[2] that is, the outskirts of the camp of Israel.

In accordance with the sacred significance which, as Balaam knew, attached to the number *seven* in the worship of Jehovah, seven altars were now built on the heights of Baal, and seven bullocks and seven rams offered upon them—a bullock and a ram on each altar. Leaving Balak and the princes of Moab by the altars, Balaam went forth in the regular heathen manner, in the hope of meeting Jehovah,[3] which is explained by Numb. xxiv. 1 as meaning "to seek auguries," such as heathen soothsayers saw in certain natural appearances or portents. And there, on the top of "a bare height,"[4] God did meet Balaam, not in auguries, but by putting "a word in Balaam's mouth." As the man shared not in it otherwise than by being the outward instrument of its communication, this "word" was to him only "a parable," and is designated as such in Scripture. Never before so clearly as in presence of the powers of heathenism, assembled to contend against Israel, did Jehovah show forth His almighty power, alike in making use of an instrument almost passive in His hand, and in disclosing His eternal purpose.[5]

[1] Tristram, p. 304.
[2] Numb. xxii. 41.
[3] Numb. xxiii. 3.
[4] So literally; Numb. xxiii. 3.
[5] The prophecies of Balaam certainly go far beyond the range of the prophetic vision of that time. Could it be, because Balaam was so entirely passive, as it were transmitting, without absorbing, any of the rays of light, nor yet mingling them with the colouring in his own mind?

FIRST "PARABLE" OF BALAAM.[1]

From Aram brought me Balak,
The king of Moab from the mountains of the east—
Come, curse me Jacob,
And come, threaten[2] Israel!
How shall I curse whom God doth not curse,
And how shall I threaten whom Jehovah threatens not?
For, from the top of the rocks I see him,
And from the hills I behold him:
Lo, a people dwelling[3] alone,
And not reckoning itself among the nations (the Gentiles)!
Who can count the dust of Jacob,
And the number of the fourth part[4] of Israel?
Let me die the death of the righteous,[5]
And let my latter end be like his!

Two things will be noted, without entering into special criticism. First, as to the form of this parable: each thought is embodied in two sentences, with rapid, almost abrupt, transitions from one thought to the other. Secondly, the outward and inward separation of Israel (the former as symbol of the latter) is singled out as the grand characteristic of God's people—a primary truth this of the Old Testament, and, in its spiritual application, of the New Testament also. But even in its literality it has proved true in the history of Israel of old, and still applies to them, showing us that Israel's history is not yet finished; that God has not forgotten His people; and that a purpose of mercy yet awaits them, in accordance with His former dealings. Such a people Balaam could not curse. On the contrary, he could only wish that his death should be like theirs whom God's ordinances and institutions kept

[1] Of course, we translate literally.
[2] Literally: pronounce wrath.
[3] We have put it so as to include both the present and the future tense.
[4] Bishop H. Browne prefers the rendering "progeny." But "the fourth part" seems to refer to the square arrangement of the camp of Israel, each side of the square being occupied by three tribes.
[5] In the *plural* number, referring to Israel.

separate outwardly, and made righteous inwardly, referring in this, of course, to Israel not as individuals, but in their totality as the people of God. In the language of a German critic,[1] "The pious Israelite could look back with calm satisfaction, in the hour of his death, upon a life rich in proofs of the blessing, forgiving, protecting, delivering, saving mercy of God. With the same calm satisfaction would he look upon his children, and children's children, in whom he lived again, and in whom also he would still take part in the high calling of his nation, and in the ultimate fulfilment of the glorious promise which it had received from God. . . . And for himself, the man who died in the consciousness of possessing the mercy and love of God, knew also that he would carry them with him as an inalienable possession, a light in the darkness of Sheol. He knew that he would be 'gathered to his fathers'—a thought which must have been a very plenteous source of consolation, of hope, and of joy."

THE SECOND "PARABLE" OF BALAAM.

It was but natural that Balak should have been equally surprised and incensed at the words of the soothsayer. The only solution he could suggest was, that a fuller view of the camp of Israel might change the disposition of the magician. "Come, I pray thee, with me unto another place, from whence thou mayest see them (viz., in their totality); only the end (utmost part) of them seest thou, but the whole of them thou seest not—and from thence curse me them."[2] The station now selected was on "the field of the watchers," on the top of Pisgah, affording not only a full view of the camp, but of the Land of Promise itself. Here Moses, not long afterwards, took his farewell prospect of the goodly heritage which the Lord had assigned to His people.[3] The same formalities as before

---

[1] Kurtz, *History of the Old Covenant*, vol. iii. p. 432, Engl. Trans.
[2] Numb. xxiii. 13. So literally; the critical discussion see in Keil, *Bible Commentary*, vol. ii. p. 313.
[3] A description of the view from Pisgah is given in a subsequent chapter.

having been gone through, in regard to altars and sacrifices, Balaam once more returned to Balak with the following message:

> Rise up, Balak, and hear,
> Hearken to me, son of Zippor!
> Not man is God that He should lie,
> Nor a son of man that He should repent!
> Hath He said, and shall He not do it,
> Hath He spoken, and shall He not fulfil it?
> Behold, to bless, I have received—
> And He hath blessed, and I cannot turn it back!
> He beholdeth not iniquity in Jacob,
> And He looketh not upon distress in Israel;
> Jehovah his God is with him,
> And the king's jubilee in the midst of him.[1]
> God bringeth them out of Egypt—
> As the unwearied strength of the buffalo is his.[2]
> For, no augury in Jacob, no soothsaying[3] in Israel,
> According to the time it is said to Jacob and to Israel what God doeth.[4]
> Behold, the people, like a lioness it riseth,
> And like a lion it raiseth itself up—
> He shall not lie down, till he has eaten the prey,[5]
> And drink the blood of the slain.

The meaning of this second "parable" needs no special explanation. Only it will be noticed, that the progress of thought is successively marked by *four lines*—the last two always expressing the ground, or showing the foundation of the two first. The centre couplet is the most important. It marks for ever, that the Covenant-Presence of God in Israel, or, as we should now express it, that the grace of God, is the ultimate cause of the forgiveness of sins, and that the happy realisation of Jehovah

---

[1] That is, the shout of jubilee on account of the abiding presence of Jehovah as their King is in the midst of the camp of Israel. This is symbolised by the blast of the trumpets, which is designated by the same word as that rendered "jubilee."

[2] Viz., Israel's.

[3] The same word by which Balaam himself is uniformly designated as "the soothsayer."

[4] In due time God reveals by His word to Israel His purpose.

[5] Literally, "the torn," what he had torn in pieces.

as the King is the ground of joy. Whenever and wherever that Presence is wanting only unforgiven sin is beheld; wherever that shout is not heard only misery is felt.

THE THIRD "PARABLE" OF BALAAM.

In his despair Balak now proposed to try the issue from yet a third locality. This time a ridge somewhat farther north was selected—"the top of Peor that looketh toward Jeshimon." A third time seven altars were built and sevenfold sacrifices offered. But there was a marked difference in the present instance. Balaam went no more "as at other times to seek for auguries."[1] Nor did Jehovah now, as formerly (xxiii. 5, 16), "put a word in his mouth." But "the Spirit of God came upon him" (xxiv. 2), in the same manner as afterwards upon Saul[2]—he was in the ecstatic state, powerless and almost unconscious, or, as Balaam himself describes it, with his *outward* eyes shut (ver. 3), and "falling," as if struck down, while seeing "the vision of the Almighty," and "having his (inner) eyes opened" (ver. 4).

> Saith Balaam, the son of Beor,
> And saith the man with closed eye,[3]
> Saith he, hearing the words of God,
> Beholding the vision of the Almighty: he beholdeth—falling down—
>   and with open eyes!
> How good are thy tabernacles, Jacob,
> Thy dwellings, O Israel—
> Like (watered) valleys they stretch, like gardens by a river,
> Like aloes Jehovah planted, like cedars by the waters.[4]
> Flow waters from his twin buckets—and his seed by many waters,
> Higher than Agag[5] shall be his king—and his kingdom be exalted.

---

[1] Numb. xxiv. 1.   [2] 1 Sam. xix. 23.
[3] The Targum Onkelos, however, renders, "the man who saw clearly."
[4] Targum Onkelos: "as rivers flowing onward; as the watered garden by Euphrates—as aromatic shrubs planted by the Lord; as cedars by the waters."
[5] *Agag*—literally, "the fiery"—was not the name of one special king (1 Sam. xv. 8), but the general designation of the kings of Amalek, as Abimelech that of the kings of Philistia, and Pharaoh of Egypt.

> God brings him from Egypt—his the unwearied strength of the buffalo—
> He shall eat the nations (Gentiles) his enemies—and their bones shall he gnaw—and his arrows shall he split.[1]
> He coucheth, lieth down like a lion and like a lioness—who shall rouse him?
> Blessed he that blesseth thee, and cursed he that curseth thee!

We can scarcely wonder that the bitter disappointment of Balak should now have broken forth in angry reproaches. But Balaam had not yet finished his task. Before leaving the king he must deliver another part of the message, which he had already received from Jehovah,[2] but not yet spoken. "Come, I will advise thee what this people shall do to thy people in the latter days" (xxiv. 14).

PROPHETIC MESSAGE THROUGH BALAAM IN FOUR "PARABLES."

First "parable," descriptive first of the "latter days," and then referring to Moab, as the representative of heathenism:

> Saith Balaam, the son of Beor, and saith the man with closed eye,
> Saith he, hearing the words of God, and knowing the knowledge of the Most High,
> Beholding the vision of the Almighty: he beholdeth—falling down—and with open eyes:
> I behold Him, but not now—I descry Him, but not nigh!
> Cometh[3] a Star from Jacob, and rises a Sceptre from Israel,
> And dasheth the two sides of Moab, and overthroweth the sons of tumult.[4]

---

[1] The rendering of this clause is exceedingly difficult and doubtful. I have taken the verb in its original meaning, *divide, split*, as in Judges v. 26, "When she had split and stricken through his temples."

[2] This we gather from the addition of the words, "knowing the knowledge of the Most High" (xxiv. 16) besides, "beholding the vision of the Almighty" (ver. 4).

[3] Literally, makes its way.

[4] Among all nations "the star" has been associated with the future glory of great kings. The application of it to the Messiah is not only constant in Scripture, but was universally acknowledged by the ancient

And Edom shall be a possession, and a possession shall be Seir[1]—his
    enemies[2]—
And Israel is doing mighty things![3]
And shall come from Jacob (a ruler)
And shall destroy what remaineth out of the cities.

Second "parable" against Amalek—as the representative of heathenism in its *first* contest against Israel:

And he beheld Amalek, and he took up his parable, and said:
First of the Gentiles Amalek—and his latter end even unto destruction.

Third "parable" in favour of the Kenites as the friends and allies of Israel:

And he beheld the Kenites, and he took up his parable, and said:
Durable thy dwelling-place, and placed on the rock thy nest.
For shall Kajin be for destruction,
Until Asshur shall lead thee away?

Fourth "parable" concerning the Assyrian empire, and the kingdoms of this world, or prophecy of "the end," appropriately beginning with a "*woe:*"

And he took up his parable, and said:[4]
Woe! who shall live when God putteth this?[5]
And ships from the side of Chittim—and afflict Asshur, and afflict
    Eber—
And he also unto destruction!

This latter may, indeed, be characterised as the most wonderful of prophecies. More than a thousand years before the event, not only the rising of the great world-empire of the West

---

Jews. Both the Targum Onkelos and that of Jonathan apply it in this manner. "The two sides of Moab," *i.e.*, from end to end of the land. "The sons of tumult," *i.e.*, the rebellious nations.

[1] Edom is the people; Seir the country.
[2] "His enemies," viz., those of Israel; the language is very abrupt.
[3] Onkelos: "prosper in riches."
[4] Of course, the Assyrian empire was as yet in the far future, and could not therefore be "beheld" like Moab, Amalek, and the Kenites.
[5] Who shall be able to abide when God doeth all this?

is here predicted, with its conquest of Asshur and Eber (*i.e*, of the descendants of Eber),[1] but far beyond this the final destruction of that world-empire is foretold! In fact, we have here a series of prophecies, commencing with the appearance of the Messiah and closing with the destruction of Anti-Christ. To this there is no parallel in Scripture, except in the visions of Daniel. No ingenuity of hostile criticism can take from, or explain away the import of this marvellous prediction.

And now the two parted—the king to go to his people, the soothsayer, as we gather from the sequel, to the tents of Midian. But we meet Balaam only too soon again. One who had entered on such a course could not stop short of the terrible end. He had sought to turn away Jehovah from His people, and failed. He would now endeavour to turn the people from Jehovah. If he succeeded in this, the consequences to Israel would be such as Balak had desired to obtain. By his advice[2] the children of Israel were seduced into idolatry and all the vile abominations connected with it.[3] In the judgment which ensued, not fewer than 24,000 Israelites perished, till the zeal of Phinehas stayed the plague, when in his representative capacity he showed that Israel, as a nation, abhorred idolatry and the sins connected with it, as the greatest crime against Jehovah. But on "the evil men and seducers" speedy judgment came. By God's command the children of Israel were avenged of the Midianites. In the universal slaughter of Midian, Balaam also perished.

The figure of Balaam stands out alone in the history of the Old Testament. The only counterpart to it is that of Judas, the traitor. Balaam represented the opposition of heathenism; Judas that of Judaism. Both went some length in following the truth; Balaam honestly acknowledged the God of Israel, and followed His directions; Judas owned the Messianic appearance in Jesus, and joined His disciples. But in the

---

[1] Gen. x. 21.   [2] Numb. xxxi. 16; Rev. ii. 14.
[3] The service of Baal-Peor represents the vilest form of idolatry. See Fürst, Dict. *sub voce*.

crisis of their inner history, when that came which, in one form or another, must be to every one the decisive question—each failed. Both had stood at the meeting and parting of the two ways, and both chose that course which rapidly ended in their destruction. Balaam had expected the service of Jehovah to be quite other from what he found it; and, trying to make it such as he imagined and wished, he not only failed, but stumbled, fell, and was broken. Judas, also, if we may be allowed the suggestion, had expected the Messiah to be quite other than he found Him; disappointment, perhaps failure in the attempt to induce Him to alter His course, and an increasingly widening gulf of distance between them, drove him, step by step, to ruin. Even the besetting sins of Balaam and of Judas—covetousness and ambition—are the same. And as, when Balaam failed in turning Jehovah from Israel, he sought—only too successfully—to turn Israel from the Lord; so when Judas could not turn the Christ from His purpose towards His people, he also succeeded in turning Israel, as a nation, from their King. In both instances, also, for a moment a light more bright than before was cast upon the scene. In the case of Balaam we have the remarkable prophetic utterances, reaching far beyond the ordinary range of prophetic vision; at the betrayal of Judas, we hear the prophetic saying of the High-priest going far beyond the knowledge of the time, that Jesus should die, not only for His own people, but for a ruined world. And, lastly, in their terrible end, they each present to us most solemn warning of the danger of missing the right answer to the great question—that of absolute and implicit submission of mind, heart, and life to the revealed Covenant-Will of God.

CHAPTER III.

The Second Census of Israel—The "Daughters of Zelophehad"—Appointment of Moses' Successor—Sacrificial Ordinances—The War against Midian—Allocation of Territory East of the Jordan—Levitical and Cities of Refuge.

(NUMB. XXVI.-XXXVI.)

BEFORE describing the closing scene of Moses' life, we may here conveniently group together brief notices of the events intervening between the judgment of "the plague" on account of Israel's sin (Numb. xxv.) and the last discourses of Moses recorded in the Book of Deuteronomy.

1. A *second census* of Israel was taken by Divine direction (Numb. xxvi.). The arrangements for it were in all probability the same as those at the *first census*, thirty-eight years before (Numb. i.).[1] The "plague" had swept away any who might yet have remained of the old doomed generation, which had come out of Egypt. At any rate, none such were now left (Numb. xxvi. 64). This may have been the reason for taking a new *census*. But its main object was in view of the approaching apportionment of the land which Israel was so soon to possess. Accordingly, the census was not taken as before (Numb. i.), according to the number of individuals in each tribe, but according to "families." This corresponded in the main[2] with the names of the grandsons and great-grandsons of Jacob, enumerated in Gen. xlvi. In reference to the future

---

[1] The results of that census, as compared with the first, have been stated in a previous volume.

[2] The reason of any divergences has been explained in the first volume of this series (*History of the Patriarchs*, p. 174).

division of the land, it was arranged that the *extent* of the "inheritance" allotted to each tribe should correspond to its numbers (Numb. xxvi. 52–54). But the exact locality assigned to each was to be determined "by lot" (vers. 55, 56), so that each tribe might feel that it had received its "possession" directly from the Lord Himself.

The proposed division of the land brought up a special question of considerable importance to Israel. It appears that one Zelophehad, of the tribe of Manasseh, and of the family of Gilead, had died—not in any special judgment, but along with the generation that perished in the wilderness. Having left no sons, his daughters were anxious to obtain a "possession," lest their father's name should be "done away from among his family" (Numb. xxvii.). By Divine direction, which Moses had sought, their request was granted,[1] and it became "a statute of judgment" in Israel—a juridical statute—that daughters, or—in their default—the nearest kinsman, should enter upon the inheritance of those who died without leaving sons. In all such cases, of course the children of those who obtained the possession would have to be incorporated, not with the tribe to which they originally belonged, but with that in which their "inheritance" lay. Thus the "name" of a man would not "be done away from among his family." Nor was this "statute" recorded merely on account of its national bearing, but for higher reasons. For this desire to preserve a name in a family in Israel sprang not merely from feelings natural in such circumstances, but was connected with the hope of the coming Messiah. Till *He* appeared, each family would fain have preserved its identity. Several instances of such changes from one tribe to another, through maternal inheritance, are recorded in Scripture (comp. 1 Chron. ii. 34, 35; Numb. xxxii. 41, and Deut. iii. 14, 15, and 1 Chron. ii. 21–23; and

---

[1] To prevent the possibility of the possession of Zelophehad passing, in the year of Jubilee, away from the tribe to which Zelophehad had belonged, it was determined (Numb. xxxvi.) that his daughters should not marry out of their father's tribe; and this was afterwards made a general law.

2. God intimated once more to Moses his impending death, before actual entrance into the Land of Promise (Numb. xxvii. 12–14). In so doing, mention of the sin which had caused this judgment was repeated, to show God's holiness and justice, even in the case of His most approved servants. On the other hand, this second reminder also manifested the faithfulness of the Lord, Who would have His servant, as it were, set his house in order, that he might meet death, not at unawares, but with full consciousness of what was before him. It is touching to see how meekly Moses received the sentence. Faithful to the end in his stewardship over God's house, his chief concern was, that God would appoint a suitable successor, so "that the congregation of the Lord be not as sheep which have no shepherd" (vers. 15–17). To this office Joshua, who had the needful spiritual qualifications, was now set apart by the laying on of Moses' hands, in presence of Eleazar the priest and of the congregation. Yet only part of Moses' "honour"— so much as was needful to ensure the obedience of Israel— was put upon Joshua, while his public movements were to be directed by "the judgment of the Urim" and Thummim. Thus did God not only vindicate the honour of His servant Moses, but also show that the office which Moses had filled was, in its nature, unique, being typical of that committed in all its fulness to the Great Head of the Church.

3. Now that the people were about to take possession of the land, the sacrificial ordinances were once more enjoined, and with full details. The daily morning and evening sacrifice had already been previously instituted in connection with the altar of burnt-offering (Ex. xxix. 38–42). To this daily consecration of Israel were now added the special sacrifices of the Sabbath—symbolical of a deeper and more special dedication, on God's own day. The Sabbatic and the other festive sacrifices were always brought in addition to the daily offering. Again, the commencement of every month was marked by a

special sacrifice, with the addition of a sin-offering, while the blast of the priests' trumpets was intended, as it were, to bring Israel's prayers and services in remembrance before the Lord. If the beginning of each month was thus significantly consecrated, the feast of unleavened bread (from the 15th to the 21st of Abib), which made that month the beginning of the year, was marked by the repetition *on each of its seven days* of the sacrifices which were prescribed for every "new moon." The Paschal feast (on the 14th of Abib) had no general congregational sacrifice, but only that of the lamb for the Paschal supper in each household. Lastly, the sacrifices for *the feast of weeks* were the same as those for the feast of unleavened bread, *with the addition* of the two "wave loaves" and their accompanying sacrifices prescribed in Lev. xxiii. 17–21.[1] This concluded the first festive cycle in the year.

The second cycle of feasts took place in the seventh or sacred month—seven being the sacred number, and that of the covenant. It began with new moon's day when, besides the daily, and the ordinary new moon's offerings, special festive sacrifices were brought (Numb. xxix. 1–6). Then on the 10th of that month was the "Day of Atonement," while on the 15th commenced the feast of tabernacles, which lasted seven days, and was followed by an octave. All these feasts had their appropriate sacrifices.[2] The laws as to sacrifices appropriately close with directions about "vows" (Numb. xxx.). In all the ordinances connected with the sacred seasons, the attentive reader will mark the symbolical significance attaching to the number *seven*—alike in the feasts themselves, in their number,

---

[1] That the sacrifices prescribed in Lev. xxiii. 17–21 were not the same as those in Numb. xxviii. 26–31, is not only established by the unanimous testimony of Jewish tradition, but appears from a comparison of the differences between the sacrifices ordained in these two passages. Thus the feast of weeks or "of first-fruits" had threefold sacrifices—the ordinary daily, the ordinary festive, and the special festive sacrifice.

[2] For details as to the manner in which these feasts were observed at the time of Christ, I have to refer the reader to my book on *The Temple its Ministry, and Services at the Time of Christ.*

their sacrifices, and in that of the days appointed for holy convocation. Indeed, the whole arrangement of time was ordered on the same principle, ascending from the Sabbath of days, to the Sabbath of weeks, of months, of years, and finally to the Sabbath of Sabbatic years, which was the year of Jubilee. And thus all time pointed forward and upward to the "Sabbatism," or sacred rest, that remaineth for "the people of God" (Heb. iv. 9).

4. All that has hitherto been described occurred *before* the expedition against Midian, by which Israel was "avenged" for the great sin into which they had by treachery been seduced. That expedition, which was accompanied by Phinehas, whose zeal had formerly stayed the plague (Numb. xxv. 7, 8), was not only completely successful, but executed all the Divine directions given. The Midianites seem to have been taken by surprise, and made no resistance. The five kings of Midian, or rather the five chieftains of their various tribes (comp. Numb. xxv. 15), all of whom seem to have been tributaries of Sihon (comp. Josh. xiii. 21), were killed, as well as the great bulk of the population, and "their cities," and "tent-villages" (erroneously rendered in the Authorised Version "goodly castles") "burnt with fire." Besides a large number of prisoners, immense booty was taken. To show their gratitude for the marvellous preservation of the people, who had probably surprised their enemies in one of their wild licentious orgies, the princes offered as an "oblation" to the sanctuary all the golden ornaments taken from the Midianites. The value of these amounted, according to the present standard of money, to considerably upwards of 25,000*l*.

The destruction of the power of Midian, who might have harassed them from the east, secured to Israel the quiet possession of the district east of Jordan, which their arms had already conquered. All along, from the river Arnon in the south, which divided Israel from Moab, to the river Jabbok and far beyond it, the land of Gilead[1] and of Bashan,

[1] Numb. xxxii. 1 speaks of "the Land of Jazer and of Gilead." "Jazer,"

their borders were safe from hostile attacks. The accounts of travellers are unanimous in describing that district as specially suited for pastoral purposes. We read of magnificent park-like scenery, of wide upland pastures, and rich forests, which everywhere gladden the eye. No wonder that those of the tribes which had all along preserved their nomadic habits, and whose flocks and herds constituted their main possessions and their wealth, should wish to settle in those plains and mountains. To them they were in very truth the land of promise, suited to their special wants, and offering the very riches which they desired. The other side Jordan had little attraction for them; and its possession would have been the opposite of advantageous to a strictly pastoral people. Accordingly, "the children of Gad," and "the children of Reuben" requested of Moses: "Let this land be given unto thy servants for a possession, and bring us not over Jordan" (Numb. xxxii. 5).

If this proposal did not actually imply that those tribes intended henceforth quietly to settle down, leaving their brethren to fight alone for the conquest of Palestine proper, it was at least open to such interpretation. Moses seems to have understood it in that sense. But, if such had been their purpose, they would not only have separated themselves from the Lord's work and leading, but, by discouraging their brethren, have re-enacted, only on a much larger scale, the sin of those unbelieving spies who, thirty-eight years before, had brought such heavy judgment upon Israel. And the words of Moses prevailed. Whether from the first their real intentions had been right, or the warning of Moses had influenced them for good, they now solemnly undertook to accompany their brethren across Jordan, and to stand by them till they also had entered on their possession. Until then they would only restore

---

or "Jaazer" (Numb. xxi. 32) was a town on the way between Heshbon in the south and Bashan in the north. It gave its name to the district, and was probably specially mentioned by the Reubenites as perhaps the township east of Jordan nearest to the camp of Israel. It is supposed to be the modern Seir—almost in a line with Jericho, east of the Jordan.

the "folds"[1] for their sheep, and rebuild the destroyed cities,[2] to afford safe dwelling-places for their wives and children, and, of course, for such of their number as were either left behind for defence, or incapable of going forth to war. On this express promise, their request was granted, and the ancient kingdoms of Sihon and of Og were provisionally assigned to Reuben, Gad, and half the tribe of Manasseh, which latter had made special conquests in Gilead (Numb. xxxii. 39). But the actual division of the district among these tribes was left over for the period when the whole country should be allocated among the children of Israel (Josh. xiii.).

5. The arrangements preparatory to possession of the land appropriately concluded with two series of ordinances.[3] The *first* of these (Numb. xxxiii. 50–xxxiv.) directed the extermination of the Canaanites and of all traces of their idolatry, re-enjoining, at the same time, the partition of the now purified land, by lot, among the tribes of Israel (Numb. xxxiii. 50–56). Next, the boundary lines of Palestine were indicated, and the persons named who were to superintend the partition of the country (Numb. xxxiv.). This duty was intrusted to Eleazar the high-priest, and to Joshua, along with ten representative "priests," one from each of the ten tribes, Reuben and Gad having already received their portion on the other side Jordan.

The *second* series of ordinances now enacted (Numb. xxxv., xxxvi.) was, if not of greater importance, yet of even deeper symbolical meaning. According to the curse that had been pronounced upon Levi, that tribe was destined to be "divided in Jacob" (Gen. xlix. 7). But, in the goodness of God, this was now converted into a blessing alike to Levi and to all

---

[1] These are not "Hazzeroth," but rubble walls for sheep, made of loose stones.

[2] These cities were rebuilt before the apportionment of the country among these two and a half tribes. This appears from the fact that, for example, *Dibon* and *Aroer* were built by "the children of Gad" (Numb. xxxii. 34, 35), but afterwards allocated to Reuben (Josh. xiii. 16, 17).

[3] Each of these two series is marked by a special preface—the first, Numb. xxxiii. 50; the second, Numb. xxxv. 1.

Israel. The Levites, the special property and election of the Lord, were to be scattered among all the other tribes, to recall by their presence everywhere the great truths which they symbolised, and to keep alive among the people the knowledge and service of the Lord. On the other hand, they were not to be quite isolated, but gathered together into cities, so that by fellowship and intercourse they might support and strengthen one another. For this purpose forty-eight cities were now assigned to the Levites—of course not exclusive of any other inhabitants, but "to dwell in," that is, they were to have as many houses in them as were required for their accommodation. Along with these houses certain "suburbs," also, or "commons" for their herds and flocks, were to be assigned them—covering in extent on each side a distance of 1000 cubits (1500 feet) round about their cities (Numb. xxxv. 4). Besides, around this inner, another outer circle of 2000 cubits was to be drawn in every direction. These were to be the fields and vineyards of the Levites[1] (ver. 5). The number of these cities in each tribe varied according to the size of its territory. Thus Judah and Simeon had to furnish nine cities, Naphtali only three, and each of the other tribes four (Josh. xxi.). Lastly, the thirteen Levitical cities in the territories of Judah, Simeon, and Benjamin were specially assigned to the priests, the descendants of the house of Aaron, while six of the Levitical cities—three east and three west of the Jordan—were set apart as "cities of refuge," for the unintentional manslayer. It is interesting to notice, that even the number of the Levitical cities was significant. They amounted in all to forty-eight, which is a multiple of four, the symbolical number of the kingdom of God in the world, and of twelve, the number of the tribes of Israel.

In regard to the "cities of refuge," for the protection of the unintending manslayer, it must not be imagined that the simple plea of unintentional homicide afforded safety. The law, indeed,

---

[1] Very varied interpretations of these two difficult verses have been proposed. That adopted in the text is in accordance with Jewish tradition, and the most simple, while it meets all the requirements of the text.

provided that the country both east and west of the Jordan should be divided in three parts—each with its "city of refuge," the roads to which were always to be kept in good repair. But, according to the sacred text (Numb. xxxv. 25, comp. Josh. xx. 4), a homicide would, on arriving at the gates of a city of refuge, first have to plead his cause before the elders of that city, when, if it approved itself to their minds, they would afford him provisional protection. If, however, afterwards, the "avenger of blood" claimed his extradition, the accused person would be sent back under proper protection to his own city, where the whole case would be thoroughly investigated. If the homicide was then proved to have been unintentional, the accused would be restored to the "city of refuge," and enjoy its protection, till the death of the high priest set him free to return to his own city.[1] As for the duty of "avenging blood," its principle is deeply rooted in the Old Testament, and traced up to the relation in which God stands to our world. For, the blood of man, who is God's image, when shed upon earth, which is God's property, "crieth" unto God (Gen. iv. 10)—claims payment like an unredeemed debt. Hence the expression "avenger of blood," which should be literally rendered "redeemer of blood." On the other hand, the symbolical meaning of the cities of refuge will readily be understood. There—in the place of God's merciful provision—the manslayer was to find a refuge, sheltered, as it were, under the wings of the grace of God, till the complete remission of the punishment at the death of the high priest—the latter symbolically pointing forward to the death of Him Whom God has anointed our great High Priest, and Who "by His one oblation of Himself once offered," hath made "a full, perfect, and sufficient sacrifice, oblation, and satisfaction" for the sins of the world.

[1] Perek II. of the Mishnic tractate *Maccoth* treats on this subject, and expounds at length the application of this law.

CHAPTER IV.

Death and Burial of Moses.

(Deut. iii. 23-29; Numb. xxvii. 15-23; Deut. xxxiv.)

ALL was now ready, and Israel about to cross the Jordan and take possession of the Promised Land! It was only natural—one of those traits in the history of the great heroes of the Bible, so peculiarly precious, as showing in their weakness their kinship to our feelings—that Moses should have longed to share in what was before Israel. Looking back the long vista of these one hundred and twenty years—first of life and trial in Egypt, then of loneliness and patient faith while feeding the flocks of Jethro, and, lastly, of labour and weariness in the wilderness, it would indeed have been strange, had he not wished now to have part in the conquest and rest of the goodly land. He had believed in it; he had preached it; he had prayed for it; he had laboured, borne, fought for it. And now within reach and view of it *must* he lay himself down to die?

Scripture records,[1] with touching simplicity, what passed between Moses and his Heavenly Father.[2] "And I entreated grace from the Lord at that time, saying: Lord Jehovah, Thou hast begun to show Thy servant Thy greatness and Thy strong hand. For what God is there in heaven or in the earth which doeth like Thy doings and like Thy might? Oh, that I might now go over and see the good land which is on the other side Jordan, this goodly mountain and the Lebanon! And Jehovah was wroth with me on account of you, and hearkened not unto me. And God said to me: Let it now

---

[1] Deut. iii. 23-26.   [2] We translate literally.

suffice thee[1]—continue not to speak to Me any more on this matter." The deep feelings of Moses had scarcely bodied themselves in the language of prayer. Rather had it been the pouring forth of his inmost desires before his Father in heaven—a precious privilege which His children possess at all times. But even so Moses had in this also, though but "as a steward" and "afar off," to follow Him whose great type he was, and to learn the peaceful rest of this experience, after a contest of thought and wish: "Nevertheless, not my will, but Thine be done." And it was the good will of God that Moses should lay himself down to rest without entering the land. Although it came in punishment of Israel's and of Moses' sin at the waters of Meribah, yet it was also better that it should be so—better for Moses himself. For on the top of Pisgah God prepared something better for Moses than even entrance into the land of earthly promise.

And now calmly, as a father setteth his house in order, did Moses prepare for his departure. During his life all his thoughts had been for Israel; and he was faithful even unto the death. His last care also had been for the people whom he had loved, and for the work to which he had been devoted—that Jehovah would provide for His congregation "a shepherd" "who may lead them out and bring them in."[2] Little else was left to be done. In a series of discourses, Moses repeated, and more fully re-stated, to Israel the laws and ordinances of God their King. His last record was "a song" of the mercy and truth of God;[3] his last words a blessing upon Israel.[4] Then, amid the respectful silence of a mourning people, he set out alone upon his last pilgrim-journey. All the way up to the highest top of Pisgah the eyes of the people must have followed him. They could watch him as he stood there in the sunset, taking his full view of the land—there to see for himself how true and faithful Jehovah had been. Still could they descry

---

[1] Literally: Enough (sufficient) for thee.   [2] Numb. xxvii. 16, 17.
[3] Deut. xxxii.   [4] Deut. xxxiii.

his figure, as, in the shadows of even, it moved towards a valley apart. After that no mortal eye ever beheld him, till, with Elijah, he stood on the mount of transfiguration. Then indeed was the longing wish of Moses, uttered many, many centuries before, fulfilled far beyond his thinking or hoping at the time. He *did* stand on "the goodly mountain" within the Land of Promise, worshipping, and giving testimony to Him in "Whom all the promises are yea and amen." It was a worthy crowning this of such a life. Not the faithful steward of Abraham, Eliezer of Damascus, when he brought to his master's son the God-given bride, could with such joy see the end of his faithful stewardship when the heir entered on his possession, as this "steward over God's house," when on that mountain he did homage to "the Son in His own house."

But to Israel down in the valley had Moses never so preached of the truth and faithfulness of Jehovah, and of His goodness and support to His people, as from the top of Pisgah. There was a strange symbolical aptness even in the ascent of the mount, 4,500 feet up, which is "rapid" but "not rugged."[1] Standing on the highest crest, the prospect would, indeed, seem almost unbounded. *Eastwards*, stretching into Arabia, rolls a boundless plain—one waving ocean of corn and grass. As the eye turns *southwards*, it ranges over the land of Moab, till it rests on the sharp outlines of Mounts Hor and Seir, and the rosy granite peaks of Arabia. To the *west* the land descends, terrace by terrace, to the Dead Sea, the western outline of which can be traced in its full extent. Deep below lies that sea, "like a long strip of molten metal, with the sun mirrored on its surface, waving and undulating in its further edge, unseen in its eastern limits, as though poured from some deep cavern beneath." Beyond it would appear the ridge of Hebron, and

---

[1] Our description here, and of the view from the top is from Canon Tristram's *Land of Israel*, pp. 539-543, of course, in a shortened form. We must content ourselves with this general acknowledgment without always the formality of inverted commas.

then as the eye travelled northwards, successively the sites of Bethlehem and of Jerusalem. The holy city itself would be within range of view—Mount Moriah, the Mount of Olives; on the one side of it the gap in the hills leading to Jericho, while on the other side, the rounded heights of Benjamin would be clearly visible. Turning *northwards*, the eye follows the winding course of Jordan from Jericho, the city of palm-trees, up the stream. Looking across it, it rests on the rounded top of Mount Gerizim, beyond which the plain of Esdraelon opens, and the shoulder of Carmel appears. That blue haze in the distance is the line of "the utmost sea." Still farther northwards rise the outlines of Tabor, Gilboa, the top of snow-clad Hermon, and the highest range of Lebanon. In front are the dark forests of Ajalon, Mount Gilead, then the land of Bashan and Bozrah. "And Jehovah shewed Moses all the land of Gilead, unto Dan, and all Naphtali, and the land of Ephraim, and Manasseh, and all the land of Judah, unto the utmost sea, and the Negeb, and the plain of the valley of Jericho, the city of palm-trees, unto Zoar."[1]

Such was the prospect which, from that mountain-top, spread before Moses. And when he had satiated his eyes upon it, he descended into that valley apart to lay him down to rest. Into the mysterious silence of that death and burial at the hands of Jehovah we dare not penetrate. Jewish tradition, rendering the expression (Deut. xxxiv. 5) literally, has it that "Moses the servant of Jehovah died there ... at the mouth of Jehovah," or, as they put it, by the kiss of the Lord. But from the brief saying of Scripture[2] may we not infer that although Moses also received in death the wages of sin, yet his body passed not through corruption, however much "the devil," contending as for his lawful prey, "disputed" for its possession, but was raised up to be with Elijah the first to welcome the Lord in His glory? For "men bury a body that it may pass into corruption. If Jehovah, therefore, would not suffer the body of Moses to be buried by men, it is but natural

[1] Deut. xxxiv. 1-3.   [2] Jude 9.

to seek for the *reason* in the fact that He did not intend to leave him to corruption."[1]

But "*there arose not a prophet since in Israel like unto Moses, whom Jehovah knew face to face, in all the signs and the wonders, which Jehovah sent him to do in the land of Egypt to Pharaoh, and to all his servants, and to all his land, and in all that mighty hand, and in all the great terror which Moses showed in the sight of all Israel.*"[2]

"AND MOSES VERILY WAS FAITHFUL IN ALL HIS HOUSE, AS A SERVANT, FOR A TESTIMONY OF THOSE THINGS WHICH WERE TO BE SPOKEN AFTER; BUT CHRIST AS A SON OVER HIS OWN HOUSE; WHOSE HOUSE ARE WE, IF WE HOLD FAST THE CONFIDENCE AND THE REJOICING OF THE HOPE FIRM UNTO THE END."[3]

CHAPTER V.

The Charge to Joshua—Despatch of the two Spies to Jericho—Rahab.

(JOSH. I, II.)

A WIDE, rich plain at the foot of the mountains of Moab, carpeted with wild flowers springing in luxuriant beauty, watered by many rivulets and rills, here and there covered by acacia trees, where birds of brightest plumage carol, and beyond, to the south, by the banks of streams, where scented oleanders rise to a height of twenty-five feet, their flower-laden boughs bending like those of the willow—such is Abel-Shittim, "the meadow of acacias." Beyond it are the fords of Jordan, and the western heights; in the distance southwards, the hills of Judæa, on which the purple light rests. Climate and vegetation are tropical, on the eastern even more than on the western

---

[1] Kurtz, *History of the Old Covenant*, vol. iii. p. 495 (English translation).
[2] Deut. xxxiv. 10-12.   [3] Heb. iii. 5, 6.

banks of the Jordan. Many memories hallow the place. Somewhere here must Elijah have smitten the waters of Jordan, that they parted, ere the fiery chariot wrapt him from the companionship of Elisha. In this district also was the scene of John's baptism, where the Saviour humbled Himself to fulfil all righteousness. And on this "meadow of acacias" did an early summer shed its softness when, about the month of March, forty years after the Exodus, the camp of Israel kept thirty days' solemn mourning for Moses (Deut. xxxiv. 8). Behind them rose that mountain-top, from which "that saint of God" had seen his last of Israel and of the goodly land, which they were so soon to possess; before them lay the Land of Promise which they were presently to enter.

Such a leader as Moses had been would Israel never more see; nor yet one with whom God had so spoken, "mouth to mouth," as a man with his friend. A feeling of loneliness and awe must have crept over the people and over their new leader, Joshua, like that which Elisha felt, when, alone, he turned him back with the mantle of Elijah that came to him from heaven, to test whether now also the waters would divide at the bidding of the Lord God of Elijah. And the faithful Covenant-God was with Joshua, as he waited, not unbelievingly, but expectantly, in that mourning camp of Abel-Shittim, for a fresh message from God. Though he had been previously designated by God, and set apart to the leadership, it was well he should so wait, not only for his own sake, but also "that the people might afterwards not hesitate gladly to follow his leadership, who had not moved a foot without the leading of God."[1] And in due time the longed-for direction came: not in doubtful language, but renewing alike the commission of Joshua and the promises to Israel. Far as the eye could reach, to the heights of Anti-Lebanon in the extreme distance, to the shores of the Great Sea, to the Euphrates in the East—all was theirs, and not a foeman should withstand them, for God would "not fail nor forsake" their leader.

[1] Calvin.

Only two things were requisite: that, in his loving obedience, the word and commands of God should be precious to Joshua; and that in strong faith he should be "very courageous." This latter command was twice repeated, as it were to indicate alike the inward courage of faith and the outward courage of deed.

That this call had found a response in the hearts not only of Joshua, but also of the people, appears from the answer of Reuben, Gad, and the half tribe of Manasseh, when reminded of their obligation to share in the impending warfare of their brethren. While professing their readiness to acknowledge in all things the authority of Joshua, they also expressly made the latter conditional on the continued direction of Jehovah, and re-echoed the Divine admonition to be "strong and of a good courage." So much does success in all we undertake depend on the assurance of faith! "For he that wavereth is like a wave of the sea driven with the wind and tossed. For let not that man think that he shall receive anything of the Lord" (James i. 6, 7).

Thus directed and encouraged, Joshua gave orders that the people should provide themselves with the necessary victuals to begin, if occasion should offer, their forward march on the third day. In point of fact, however, it was at least five days before that movement could be made. For Joshua had deemed it prudent to adopt proper preparatory measures, although, or rather just because he was assured of Divine help, and trusted in it. Accordingly he had sent, unknown to the people,[1] two spies "to view the land and Jericho."[2] The reason of this secrecy lay probably both in the nature of their errand, and in the sad remembrance of the discouragement which evil report by the spies had formerly wrought among the people (Numb. xiv. 1). As the two spies

---

[1] In Josh. ii. 1, the accentuation connects the words "secretly" and "saying," which are separated by commas in our Authorised Version, showing that the commission was intrusted to them secretly.

[2] The meaning really is "especially Jericho," which fortress was the key to the western bank of Jordan.

stealthily crept up the eight miles of country from the western bank of the Jordan to "the city of palm trees," they must have been struck with the extraordinary "beauty and luxuriance of the district. Even now there is a bright green oasis of several miles square which marks the more rich and populous groves of Jericho."[1] Its vegetation is most rich and rare; almost every tree is tenanted by the bulbul or Palestinian nightingale, with the "hopping thrush," "the gorgeous Indian blue kingfisher, the Egyptian turtle-dove, and other singing birds of Indian or Abyssinian affinity." "On the plain above are the desert larks and chats, while half an hour's walk takes us to the Mount of Temptation, the home of the griffon, where beautifully plumed partridges, rock-swallows, rock-doves, and other birds abound. But, beyond all others, Jericho is the home of the lovely sun-bird, ... resplendent with all the colours of the humming-bird"—its back brilliant green, its throat blue, and its breast purple, "with a tuft of rich red, orange, and yellow feathers at each shoulder." The little stream—which Elisha healed from its after curse—swarms with fish, while climate and prospect are equally delicious in that early summer-like spring, when the spies visited it. And what the wealth and beauty of this plain must have been when it was crowded with feathery palms, and scented balsam gardens, we learn from the descriptions of Josephus (*Ant.* xv. 4, 2). This paradise of Canaan was guarded by the fortress of Jericho—one of the strongest in the whole land.[2] Behind its walls and battlements immense wealth was stored, partly natural and partly the result of civilisation and luxury. This appears even from the character and value of the spoil which one individual—Achan—could secrete from it (Josh. vii. 21).

As the spies neared the city, the setting sun was casting his rays in richest variegated colouring on the limestone mountains which surrounded the ancient Jericho like an amphitheatre,

---

[1] Tristram, *Land of Israel*, pp. 203 and following.

[2] This impression is irresistibly conveyed to the mind by a comparison of the Scriptural account of Jericho with that of the other cities in Canaan.

rising closest, and to the height of from 1200 to 1500 feet, in the north, where they bear the name of *Quarantania*, marking the traditional site of the forty days of our Lord's temptation; and thence stretching with widening sweep towards the south. Friend or ally there was none in that city, whose hospitality the two Israelites might have sought. To have resorted to a khan or inn would have been to court the publicity which most of all they wished to avoid. Under these circumstances, the choice of the house of Rahab, the harlot, was certainly the wisest for their purpose. But even so, in the excited state of the public mind, when, as we know (Josh. ii. 11), the terror of Israel had fallen upon all, the arrival of two suspicious-looking strangers could not remain a secret. So soon as the gates were shut, and escape seemed impossible, the king sent to make captives of what he rightly judged to be Israelitish spies. But Rahab had anticipated him. Arriving at the same conclusion as the king, and expecting what would happen, she had "hid them"—perhaps hastily—"with the stalks of flax which she had laid in order upon the roof," after the common Eastern fashion of drying flax on the flat roofs of houses. By the adroit admission of the fact that two men, previously unknown to her, had indeed come, to which she added the false statement that they had with equal abruptness left just before the closing of the gates, she succeeded in misleading the messengers of the king. The story of Rahab sounded likely enough; she had seemingly been frank, nor was there any apparent motive for untruthfulness on her part, but quite the opposite, as the same danger threatened all the inhabitants of Jericho. As Rahab had suggested, the messengers "pursued quickly" in the supposed wake of the Jewish emissaries, which would have been "the way to Jordan, unto the fords," by which they must return to the camp of Israel, and the gates were again shut, to make escape from Jericho impossible, if, after all, they had not quitted the city.

Thus far the device of Rahab had succeeded. So soon as night settled upon the city, she repaired to the roof, and acquainted the spies, who were ignorant of any danger, with what had taken place. At the same time she explained the motives of her conduct. They must indeed have listened with wonder, not unmingled with adoring gratitude, as she told them how they, in Canaan, had heard what Jehovah had done for Israel at the Red Sea, and that, by His help, the two powerful kings of the Amorites had been "utterly destroyed." The very language, in which Rahab described the terror that had fallen upon her countrymen, was the same as that uttered prophetically forty years before, when Moses and the children of Israel sang the new song on the other side of the Red Sea, Ex. xv. 14–16 (comp. Ex. xxiii. 27; Deut. ii. 25; xi. 25). But the effect of this knowledge of Jehovah's great doings differed according to the state of mind of those who heard of them. In the Canaanites it called forth the energy of despair in resisting Israel, or rather Israel's God. But in Rahab's heart it awakened far other feelings. She knew that Jehovah had given to Israel the land—and far better than even this, that "Jehovah your God, He is God in heaven above and in earth beneath." Knowing God's purpose, she would shelter the spies, and so further their errand; knowing that He alone was God, she and all near and dear to her must not take part in the daring resistance of her countrymen, but seek safety by separating themselves from them and joining the people of God. And so she implored mercy for herself and her kindred in the day when Jehovah would surely give Israel the victory. Such a request could not be refused, evidenced as its genuineness had been by her "works." The two spies solemnly acceded to it, but on condition that she would prove true to the end, helping on their work by still keeping their mission secret, and evidencing her faith by gathering on the day of trial all her kindred within her house. That house should be distinguished from all other dwellings in Jericho by exhibiting the same "scarlet cord," with which she let down the spies over the city wall upon which her house was built. All throughout, this story is full of deepest symbolical meaning. And in truth, one, prepared so to act, was in heart "an Israelite indeed," and her household already belonged to the "household of faith."

We are now in circumstances to appreciate the faith by which the harlot Rahab perished not with them that were disobedient,[1] when she had "received the spies with peace," a faith which, as St. James argues, evidenced itself "by works" (James ii. 25). In so doing, it is not necessary either to represent her in her former life as other than she really was,[2] or even to extenuate her sin in returning a false answer to the king of Jericho. Nor, on the other hand, do we wish to exaggerate the spiritual condition to which she had attained. Remembering who, and what, and among whom she had been all her life-time, her emphatic confession, that Jehovah, the God of Israel, "He is God in heaven above, and in earth beneath;" her unwavering faith in the truth of His promises, which moved her to self-denying action at such danger and sacrifice, and supported her in it; her separation from her countrymen; her conduct towards the spies at the risk of her life—all show her to have had that faith which "is the substance of things hoped for, the evidence of things unseen;" not a "dead faith," "without works," but one which "wrought with her works, and by works was made perfect." And He Who "giveth more grace" to them who wisely use what they have, marvellously owned and blessed this "firstfruits" from among the Gentiles. Her history, which, in all its circumstances, bears a remarkable analogy to that of the woman of Samaria (John iv.), is recorded for the instruction of the Church. And, as in the case of the Hebrew midwives who had preserved Israel (Ex. i. 21), God also "made her a house." She became the wife of Salmon, a prince of the tribe of Judah, and from her sprang in direct line both David (Ruth iv. 21) and David's Lord (Matt. i. 4).[3]

---

[1] Heb. xi. 31, marginal rendering.

[2] So Josephus and the Rabbis, who represent her as simply an innkeeper.

[3] The learned reader who is curious to know the Rabbinical fables about

But as for the two Israelitish spies, they hid themselves, according to Rahab's advice, for three days among the limestone caves and grottoes which abound in Mount Quarantania, while their pursuers vainly searched for them in the opposite direction of the fords of Jordan. When the fruitless pursuit had ceased, they made their way back to Joshua, expressing to him their conviction, as the result of their mission: "Truly Jehovah hath delivered into our hands all the land; for even all the inhabitants of the country do faint because of us."

CHAPTER VI.

Miraculous Parting of the Jordan, and the Passage of the Children of Israel—Gilgal and its meaning—The first Passover on the soil of Palestine.

(JOSH. III.-V. 12.)

THE morrow after the return of the spies, the camp at Shittim was broken up, and the host of Israel moved forward. It consisted of all those tribes who were to have their possessions west of the Jordan, along with forty thousand chosen warriors from Reuben, Gad, and the half tribe of Manasseh.[1] A short march brought them to the brink of Jordan. Strictly speaking, the Jordan has a threefold bank; the largest at the water's edge, which, in spring, is frequently inundated, owing to the melting of snow on Hermon; a middle bank, which is covered with rich vegetation, and an upper

---

Rahab, will find them in Lightfoot, *Hor. Hebr. et Talmud.*; and in Wetstein, *Nov. Test.*, in the notes on Matt. i. 5; also in Meuschen, *Nov. Test. ex Talm. illustr.*, p. 40.

[1] As, according to Numb. xxvi. 7, 18, 34, the total number of the men of war in the tribes Reuben and Gad, and those of half Manasseh amounted to 110,580, it follows that 70,580 must have been left behind for the protection of the territory east of the Jordan.

bank, which overhangs the river. The people now halted for three days, first to await the Divine direction as to the passage of the river, and then to prepare for receiving in a proper spirit the manifestation of Divine power about to be manifested in the miraculous parting of Jordan. For, as one has remarked, the expression used by Joshua, "the living God is among you" (Josh. iii. 10), does not merely imply the presence of God among Israel, but, as the event proved, the operations by which He shows Himself both *living* and *true*.

All that was to be done by Israel was Divinely indicated to Joshua, and all was done exactly as it had been[1] directed. First, proclamation was made throughout Israel to "sanctify" themselves, and that not only outwardly by symbolic rites, but also inwardly by turning unto the Lord, in expectant faith of "the wonders" about to be enacted. These were intimated to them beforehand (Josh. iii. 5, 13). Thus passed three days. It was "the tenth day of the first month" (Josh. iv. 19), the anniversary of the day on which forty years before Israel had set apart their Paschal lambs (Ex. xii. 3), that the miraculous passage of the Jordan was accomplished, and Israel stood on the very soil of the promised land. Before the evening of that anniversary had closed in, the memorial stones were set up in Gilgal. All between those two anniversaries seemed only as a grand historical parenthesis. But the kingdom of God has no blanks or interruptions in its history; there is a grand unity in its course, for Jehovah reigneth. With feelings stirred by such remembrances, and the expectancy of the great miracle to come, did Israel now move forward. First went the Ark, borne by the priests, and, at a reverent distance of 2000 cubits, followed the host. For, it was the Ark of the Covenant which was to make a way for Israel through the waters of Jordan, and they were to keep it in sight, so as to mark the miraculous road, as it

---

[1] We mark in this narrative *three sections*, each commencing with a Divine command (Josh. iii. 7, 8; iv. 2, 3; and iv. 15, 16), followed by Joshua's communication thereof to the people, and an account of its execution. This to connect each stage with the Lord Himself.

was gradually opened to them. It is to this that the Divine words refer (Josh. iii. 4) : " that ye may know," or rather come to know, recognise, understand, " the way by which ye must go: for ye have not passed this way heretofore." With the exception of Caleb and Joshua, none, at least of the laity,[1] had been grown up at the time, and seen it, when the Lord parted the waters of the Red Sea at the Exodus. Then it had been the uplifted wonder-working rod of Moses by which the waters were parted But now it was the Ark at whose advance they were stayed. And the difference of the means was quite in accordance with that of the circumstances. For now the Ark of the Covenant was the ordinary symbol of the Divine Presence among Israel; and God commonly employs the ordinary means of grace for the accomplishment of His marvellous purposes of mercy.

It was early spring, in that tropical district the time of early harvest (Josh iii. 15), and the Jordan had overflown its lowest banks. As at a distance of about half a mile the Israelites looked down, they saw that, when the feet of those who bore the Ark touched the waters, they were arrested."[2] Far up " beyond where they stood, at the city of Adam that is beside Zarethan,"[3] did the Divine Hand draw up the waters of Jordan, while the waters below that point were speedily drained into the Dead Sea. In the middle of the river-bed the priests with the Ark[4] halted till the whole people had passed over dryshod. Then twelve men, who had previously been detailed for the

---

[1] See *The Exodus and the Wanderings in the Wilderness*, p. 168.

[2] In Josh. iii. 11 and 13 it is significantly designated, "the Ark of Jehovah, the Lord of all the earth," as Calvin remarks, to show the subjection of all to God, and to increase the trust of Israel.

[3] This, and not, as in our Authorised Version, "very far from the city of Adam," is the correct rendering. The sites of these two cities have not been identified. From the nature of the banks, the inundation caused by this miracle would not lead to serious consequences.

[4] The attentive reader will notice that, throughout the Scripture narrative, the main stress is laid on the presence of the Ark, the priests being only introduced as the bearers of it.

purpose,[1] took up twelve large stones from where the priests had stood in the river-bed, to erect them a solemn memorial to all times of that wondrous event. Only after that did the priests come up from Jordan. And when "the soles of the priests' feet were lifted up unto the dry land" (literally, were detached, viz., from the clogging mud, "upon the dry"), "the waters of Jordan returned unto their place, and flowed over all his banks, as before." It must have been towards evening when the rest of the march was accomplished—a distance of about five miles—and Israel's camp was pitched at what afterwards became *Gilgal,* "in the east border of Jericho," about two miles from the latter city.[2]

The object and meaning of this "notable miracle" are clearly indicated in the sacred text. We know that it was as absolutely necessary in the circumstances as formerly the cleaving of the Red Sea had been. For, at that season of the year, and with the means at their disposal, it would have been absolutely impossible for a large host with women and children to cross the Jordan. But, besides, it was fitting that a miracle similar to that of the Exodus from Egypt should mark the entrance into the Land of Promise; fitting also, that the commencement of Joshua's ministry should be thus Divinely attested like that of Moses (Josh. iii. 7). Finally, it would be to Israel a glorious pledge of future victory in the might of their God (ver. 10), while to their enemies it was a sure token of the judgment about to overtake them (Josh. v. 1).

Two things yet remained to be done, before Israel could enter upon the war with Canaan. Although the people of God, Israel had been under judgment for nearly forty years, and those born in the wilderness bore not the covenant mark of circumcision. To renew that rite in their case was the

---

[1] The rendering of Josh. iv. 1-3 in our Authorised Version does not give that impression, but alike Rabbinical and the best Christian authorities regard these verses as a parenthesis, and translate, in ver. 1, "and the Lord had spoken to Joshua."

[2] Tristram, *Land of Israel,* p. 219.

first necessity, so as to restore Israel to its full position as the covenant-people of God.[1] After that, a privilege awaited Israel which for thirty-eight years they had not enjoyed. Probably the Passover at the foot of Sinai (Numb. ix. 1) had been the last, as that feast would not have been observed by the people in their uncircumcision. But at Gilgal their reproach was "rolled away," and the people of God renewed the festive remembrance of their deliverance from Egypt. Truly, that first Passover on the soil of Palestine had a twofold meaning. Even the circumstances recalled its first celebration. As the night of the first Passover was one of terror and judgment to Egypt, so now, within view of the festive camp of Gilgal, " Jericho was straitly shut up because of the children of Israel: none went out, and none came in" (Josh. vi. 1). And now also the Divine wilderness-provision of the "manna which had clung to them with the tenacity of all God's mercies," ceased on "the morrow after they had eaten of the old corn of the land: neither had the children of Israel manna any more; but they did eat of the fruits of the land of Canaan that year." And so also have miraculous gifts ceased in the Church, because their continuance has become unnecessary. Similarly will our manna-provision for daily life-need cease, when we at the last enter upon the land of promise, and for ever enjoy its fruits!

[1] Of course, the survivors of those who, having come out from Egypt, were at the time of the sentence in Kadesh under twenty years old (Numb. xiv. 29)—in short, all in Gilgal who were thirty-eight years and upwards—*had been* circumcised. Reckoning the total of males at Gilgal at about one million, the proportion of the circumcised to the uncircumcised would have been about 280,000 to 720,000. The former would suffice to prepare the Paschal lambs, and, if needful, to defend the camp at Gilgal, although the terror consequent upon the dividing of Jordan would probably have protected Israel from all hostile attacks. See Keil, *Bibl Comm.*, vol. ii. pp. 38, 39.

CHAPTER VII.

The "Prince of the Host of Jehovah" appears to Joshua—The miraculous fall of Jericho before the Ark of Jehovah.

(JOSH. v. 13; vi. 27).

AT first sight it may seem strange, that, when such fear had fallen upon the people of the land, any attempt should have been made to defend Jericho. But a fuller consideration will help us not only to understand this, but also by-and-by to see special reasons, why this one fortress should have been miraculously given to Israel. Not to mention motives of honour, which would at least have some influence with the men of Jericho, it was one of the main principles of heathenism, that each of their "gods many" was limited in his activity to one special object. But what the Canaanites had heard of Jehovah showed Him to be the God of nature, who clave the Red Sea and arrested the waters of Jordan, and that He was so far also the God of battles, as to give Israel the victory over the Amorite kings. But was His strength also the same as against their gods in reducing strong fortresses? Of that at any rate they had no experience. Trivial as such a question may sound in our ears, we have evidence that it was seriously entertained by heathendom. To mention only one instance, we know that a similar suggestion was made at a much later period, not by obscure men, but by the servants and trusted advisers of Ben-hadad, and that it was acted upon by that monarch in the belief that "Jehovah is God of the hills, but he is not God of the valleys" (1 Kings xx. 28). At any rate, it was worth the trial, and Jericho, as already stated, was the strongest fortress in Canaan, and the key to the whole country.

This latter consideration could not but have weighed on the mind of Joshua, as from the camp of Gilgal he "viewed the city." As yet no special direction had been given him how to attack Jericho, and, assuredly, the people whom he commanded were untrained for such work. While such thoughts were busy within him, of a sudden, "as he lifted up his eyes and looked, there stood over against him," not the beleaguered city, but "a man with his sword drawn in his hand." Challenged by Joshua: "Art thou for us, or for our adversaries?" the strange warrior replied: "No! But I am the Captain (or Prince) of the host of Jehovah, now I am come."[1] Here His speech was interrupted—for Joshua fell on his face before Him, and reverently inquired His commands. The reply: "Loose thy shoe from off thy foot, for the place whereon thou standest is holy,"[2] must have convinced Joshua that this Prince of the host of Jehovah was none other than the Angel of the Covenant, Who had spoken to Moses out of the burning bush (Ex. iii. 4), and Who was co-equal with Jehovah. Indeed, shortly afterwards, we find Him expressly spoken of as Jehovah (Josh. vi. 2). So then the mission of Joshua was substantially the continuation and completion of that of Moses. As at the commencement of the latter, the Angel of the Covenant had appeared and spoken out of the burning bush, so He now also appeared to Joshua, while the symbolical act of "loosing the shoe off his foot," in reverent acknowledgment of the Holy One of Israel, recalled the vision of Moses, and at the same time connected it with that of his successor. Having assured Joshua of complete victory, the Angel of Jehovah gave him detailed directions how Israel was to compass Jericho, under the leadership of the Ark of the Lord, and how, when the wall of the city had fallen, the people were to act. Implicit obedience

---

[1] This is the correct rendering of Josh. v. 14; that in our Authorised Version does not fully express the pictorial import of the original.

[2] For an explanation of the meaning of this symbol, see *The Exodus*, etc.

of what in its nature was symbolical, was absolutely requisite, and Joshua communicated the command of the Lord both to priests and people.

And now a marvellous sight would be witnessed from the walls of Jericho. Day by day, a solemn procession left the camp of Israel. First came lightly armed men,[1] then followed seven priests blowing continually, not the customary silver trumpets, but large horns, the loud sound of which penetrated to the far distance, such as had been heard at Sinai (Ex. xix. 16, 19; xx. 18). The same kind of horns were to be used on the first day of the seventh month (Lev. xxiii. 24), and to announce the year of Jubilee (Lev. xxv. 9). Thus heralded, came the Ark of Jehovah, borne by the priests, and after it "the rereward" of Israel. So they did for six days, each day once encompassing the walls of Jericho, but in solemn silence, save for the short sharp tones, or the long-drawn blasts of the priests' horns. The impression made by this long, solemn procession, which appeared and disappeared, and did its work, in solemn silence, only broken by the loud shrill notes of the horns, must have been peculiar. At length came the seventh day. Its work began earlier than on the others—"about the dawning of the day." In the same order as before, they encompassed the city, only now seven times. "And it came to pass at the seventh time, when the priests blew with the trumpets, Joshua said unto the people, Shout; for Jehovah hath given you the city." "And it came to pass, when the people heard the sound of the trumpet, and the people shouted with a great shout, that the wall fell down flat, so that the people went up into the city, every man straight before him, and they took the city." As for Jericho itself, Joshua had by Divine command declared it "*cherem*," or "devoted" to Jehovah

[1] Josh. vi. 9 implies that the host of Israel was divided into two parts: "the armed men" preceding, and "the rereward following the Ark." As the Hebrew "for armed men" is the same term as that in Josh. iv. 13 ("prepared for war"), it has been suggested by Rabbinical interpreters that "the armed men" consisted of Reuben, Gad, and the half tribe of Manasseh.

(Josh. vi. 17). In such cases, according to Lev. xxvii. 28, 29, no redemption was possible, but, as indicated in Deut. xiii. 16, alike the inhabitants and all the spoil of the city was to be destroyed, "only the silver, and the gold, and the vessels of brass and of iron" being reserved and "put into the treasury of the house of Jehovah" (Josh. vi. 24; comp. Numb. xxxi. 22, 23, 50–54). This was not the ordinary sentence against *all* the cities of Canaan. In all other cases the inhabitants alone were "smitten with the edge of the sword" (Josh. viii. 26; x. 28; comp. Deut. ii. 34; iii. 6; viii. 2; xx. 16), while the cattle and the spoil were preserved. But in the case of Jericho, for reasons to be afterwards stated, the whole city, with *all* that it contained, was *cherem*. Only Rahab, "and her father's household, and all that she had," were saved from the general wreck.

It lies on the surface of the Scriptural narrative that "a notable miracle," unparalleled in history, had in this case been "wrought" by Jehovah for Israel. As a German writer puts it: It would have been impossible to show it more clearly, that Jehovah had *given* the city to Israel. First, the river was made to recede, to allow them entrance into the land; and now the walls of the city were made to fall, to give them admission to its first and strongest city. Now such proofs of the presence and help of Jehovah, so soon after Moses' death, must have convinced the most carnal among Israel, that the same God who had cleft the Red Sea before their fathers was still on their side. And in this light must the event also have been viewed by the people of Canaan. But, besides, a deeper symbolical meaning attached to all that had happened. The first and strongest fortress in the land Jehovah God bestowed upon His people, so to speak, as a free gift, without their having to make any effort, or to run any risk in taking it. A precious pledge this of the ease with which all His gracious promises were to be fulfilled. Similarly, the manner in which Israel obtained possession of Jericho was deeply significant. Evidently, the walls of Jericho fell, not before Israel, but before the Ark of Jehovah, or rather, as it is expressly said in Josh. vi. 8, before Jehovah Himself, whose presence among His people was connected with the Ark of the Covenant. And the blast of those jubilee-horns all around the doomed city made proclamation of Jehovah, and was, so to speak, the summons of His kingdom, proclaiming that the labour and sorrow of His people were at an end, and they about to enter upon their inheritance. This was the symbolical and typical import of the blasts of the jubilee-horns, whenever they were blown. Hence also alike in the visions of the prophets and in the New Testament the final advent of the kingdom of God is heralded by the trumpet-sound of His angelic messengers (comp. 1 Cor. xv. 52; 1 Thess. iv. 16; Rev. xx. and xxi.). But, on the other hand, the advent of the kingdom of God always implies destruction to His enemies. Accordingly, the walls of Jericho must fall, and all the city be destroyed. Nor will the reader of this history fail here also to notice the significance of the number *seven*—seven horns, seven priests, seven days of compassing the walls, repeated seven times on the seventh day! The *suddenness* of the ruin of Jericho, which typified the kingdom of this world in its opposition to that of God, has also its counterpart at the end of the present dispensation. For "the day of the Lord cometh as a thief in the night; and when they shall say, Peace and safety, then sudden destruction cometh upon them, as travail upon a woman with child; and they shall not escape."

Lastly, it was fitting that Jericho should have been *entirely* devoted unto the Lord; not only that Israel might gain no immediate spoil by what the Lord had done, but also because the city, as the firstfruits of the conquest of the land, belonged unto Jehovah, just as all the first, both in His people and in all that was theirs, was His—in token that the whole was really God's property, Who gave everything to His people, and at Whose hands they held their possessions. But, to indicate the state of heart and mind with which Israel compassed the city, following the Ark in solemn silence, we recall this emphatic testimony of Scripture (Heb. xi. 30): "By faith the walls of Jericho fell down, after they were compassed about seven days." In this instance also, as just before the Lord cleft the Red Sea, and again afterwards, when in answer to Jehoshaphat's prayer God destroyed the heathen combination against His people, the Divine call to them was, "Stand ye still" (in expectant faith) "and see the salvation of Jehovah" (Ex. xiv. 13, 2 Chron. xx. 17). And so it ever is to His believing people in similar circumstances.

CHAPTER VIII.

Unsuccessful Attack upon Ai—Achan's Sin, and Judgment—Ai attacked a second time and taken.

(JOSH. VII.–VIII. 29.)

THE conquest of Jericho without fight on the part of Israel had given them full pledge of future success. But, on the other hand, also, might it become a source of greatest danger, if the gracious promises of God were regarded as national rights, and the presence of Jehovah as secured, irrespective of the bearing of Israel towards Him. It was therefore of the utmost importance, that from the first it should appear that victory over the enemy was Israel's only so long as the people were faithful to the covenant of their God.

In their progress towards the interior of the land, the fortress next to be taken was *Ai*. Broken up as the country seems to have been into small territories, each under an independent chieftain or "king," who reigned in his fortified city and held sway over the district around,[1] a series of sieges rather than of pitched battles was to be expected. *Ai*, situated on a

---

[1] In Josh. xii. 7-24, no less than thirty-one such "kings" are enumerated, as vanquished by Joshua. And it must be remembered that their territories did not by any means cover the whole of Palestine west of the Jordan.

conical hill about ten miles to the west of Jericho, was a comparatively smaller city, numbering only 12,000 inhabitants (Josh. viii. 25). Yet its position was exceedingly important. Southwards it opened the road to Jerusalem, which is only a few hours distant; northwards it commanded access to the heart of the country, so that, as we find in the sequel, a victorious army could march thence unopposed into the fertile district of Samaria. Moreover, the fate of Ai virtually decided also that of Bethel. The latter city, ruled by another independent "king,"[1] lay to the west of Ai, being separated from it by a high intervening hill. This hill, about midway between Bethel and Ai, possessed special interest. It was the site of Abram's altar, when he first entered the land (Gen. xii. 8). Here also had the patriarch stood with Lot, overlooking in the near distance the rich luxuriance of the Jordan valley, when Lot made his fatal choice of residence (Gen. xiii. 4, 10). Standing on this hill, a valley is seen to stretch westward to Bethel, while eastward, around Ai, "the wadys which at first break down steeply ... descend gradually for about three quarters of a mile, before taking their final plunge to the Jordan valley. The gently sloping ground is well studded with olive trees."[2] This rapid sketch of the locality will help us to realise the events about to be recorded.

The advance now to be made by Israel was so important, that Joshua deemed it a proper precaution to send "men to view Ai." Their report satisfied him that only an army-corps of about 3000 men was requisite to take that city. But the

[1] Josh. xii. 16. From the position of the king of Bethel in the list of vanquished "kings," we are led to infer that Bethel was taken somewhat later than Ai. But, from Josh. viii. 17, we learn that there was a league between the two cities. Their armies must have either moved in accord, or have been at the disposal of the king of Ai. In either case the men of Bethel may have made their way back to their own city when Israel turned against Ai.

[2] We are here indebted to a very interesting paper by Canon Williams, read before the Church Congress at Dublin in 1868, and to Capt. Wilson's Notes upon it.

expedition proved far from successful. The men of Ai issued from the city, and routed Israel, killing thirty-six men, pursuing the fugitives as far as "Shebarim" ("mines," or perhaps "quarries" where stones are broken), and smiting them "in the going down," that is, to about a mile's distance, where the wadys, descending from Ai, take "their final plunge" eastwards. Viewed in any light, the event was terribly ominous. It had been Israel's first fight west of the Jordan—and their first defeat. The immediate danger likely to accrue was a combination of all their enemies round about, and the utter destruction of a host which had become dispirited. But there was even a more serious aspect than this. Had God's pledged promises now failed? or, if this could not even for a moment be entertained, had the Lord given up His gracious purpose, His covenant with Israel, and the manifestation of His "Name" among all nations, connected therewith?[1] Feelings like these found expression in Joshua's appeal to God, when, with rent clothes and ashes upon their heads, he and the elders of Israel lay the livelong day, in humiliation and prayer, before the Lord, while in the camp "the hearts of the people" had "melted and became as water." We require to keep in view this contrast between the impotent terror of the people and the praying attitude of their leaders, to realise the circumstances of the case; the perplexity, the anxiety, and the difficulties of Joshua, before we judge of the language which he used. It fell indeed far short of the calm confidence of a Moses; yet, in its inquiry into the reason of God's dealings, which were acknowledged, faith, so to speak, wrestled with doubt (Josh. vii. 7), while rising fear was confronted by trust in God's promises (ver. 9). Best of all, the inward contest found expression in prayer. It was therefore, after all, a contest of faith, and faith is "the victory over the world."

Strange, that amidst this universal agitation, one should have remained unmoved, who, all the time, knew that he was the cause of Israel's disaster and of the mourning around. Yet his

---

[1] See the remarks on Ex. vi. 3 in *The Exodus, etc.*

conscience must have told him that, so long as it remained, the curse of his sin would follow his brethren, and smite them with impotence. It is this hardness of impenitence—itself the consequence of sin—which, when properly considered, vindicates, or rather demonstrates, the rightness of the Divine sentence afterwards executed upon Achan.[1] His sin was of no ordinary character. It had not only been a violation of God's express command, but daring sacrilege and profanation. And this under circumstances of the most aggravated character. Besides, Joshua had, just before the fall of Jericho, warned the people of the danger to themselves and to all Israel of taking "of the accursed thing" (Josh. vi. 18). So emphatic had been the ban pronounced upon the doomed city, that it was extended to all time, and even over the whole family of any who should presume to restore Jericho as a fortress (vi. 26).[2] And, in face of all this, Achan had allowed himself to be tempted! He had yielded to the lowest passion. One of those Babylonish garments, curiously woven with figures and pictures (such as classical writers describe), a massive golden ornament, in the shape of a tongue, and a sum of silver, amounting to about 25*l.* in a city the walls of which had just miraculously fallen before the Lord, had induced him to commit this daring sin! More than that, when it had come

---

[1] The Divine sentence needs no justification. Achan's was a sin which involved its peculiar punishment. But, as in the case of Esau, his history showed the fitness of the Divine sentence which debarred him of the "inheritance" of the promise, so was it also in the case of Achan. In studying the history of *events* we are too apt to overlook that of *persons* and *characters*.

[2] It is a common mistake to suppose that Jericho was never to be rebuilt. This evidently could not have been the meaning of Joshua, as among other cities he assigned Jericho to the tribe of Benjamin (Josh. xviii. 21). Similarly, we read of "the city of palm-trees" in Judges iii. 13, and by its own name in 2 Sam. x. 5. The ban of Joshua referred not to the rebuilding of Jericho, but to *its restoration as a fortified city*. This also appears from the terms used by Joshua ("set up the gates of it," Josh. vi. 26), and again reiterated when the threatened judgment afterwards came upon the family of Hiel (1 Kings xvi. 34).

true, as Joshua predicted (vi. 18), that such theft would "make the camp of Israel a curse, and trouble it," Achan had still persisted in his sin.

It will be remembered that, forty years before, at the brink of the Red Sea, "the Lord said unto Moses: Wherefore criest thou unto Me? speak unto the children of Israel, that they go forward!" (Ex. xiv. 15). As then, so now, when Joshua and the elders of Israel lay on their faces before the Lord, not prayer, but action was required. In the one case it was not exercise of faith to pray where *obedience* was called for; nor yet, in the other, had prayer any meaning, nor could it expect an answer, while sin remained unremoved. And so it ever is. The cause of Israel's disaster lay, not in want of faithfulness on the part of the Lord, but on that of Israel. Their sin must now be searched out, and "the accursed" be "destroyed from among them." For, although the sin of Achan was that of an individual, it involved all Israel in its guilt. The sinner was of Israel, and his sin was in Israel's camp. It is needless here to discuss the question, how one guilty of sin should involve in its consequences those connected with him, whether by family or social ties. It is simply a *fact*, admitting no discussion, and is equally witnessed when God's law in nature, and when His moral law is set at defiance. The deepest reason of it lies, indeed, in this, that the God of nature and of grace is also the founder of society; for, the family and society are not of man's devising, but of God's institution, and form part of His general plan. Accordingly, God deals with us not merely as individuals, but also as families and as nations. To question the rightness of this would be to question alike the administration, the fundamental principles, and the plan of God's universe. But there is reason for devout thankfulness, that we can, and do recognise the presence of God in both nature and in history. The highest instance of the application of this law, is that which has rendered our salvation possible. For just as we had sinned and destroyed ourselves through our connection with the first Adam, so are we saved through the second Adam—the Lord from heaven, Who has become our Substitute, that in Him we might receive the adoption of children.

The tidings, that the sin of one of their number had involved Israel in judgment, must have rapidly spread through the camp of Israel. But even this knowledge and the summons to sanctify themselves, that on the morrow the transgressor might be designated by the Lord, did not move Achan to repentance and confession. And now all Israel were gathered before the Lord. First approached the princes of the twelve tribes. Each name of a tribe had been written separately,[1] when "the lot" that "came up," or was drawn, bore the name of Judah. Thus singled out, the heads of the various clans of Judah next presented themselves, when the lot designated that of Zarhi. And still the solemn trial went on, with increasing solemnity, as the circle narrowed, when successively the families of Zabdi, and finally, among them, the household of Achan was singled out by the hand of God. All this time had Achan kept silence. And now he stood alone before God and Israel, that guilty one who had "troubled" all. Would he at the last confess, and "give glory to Jehovah" by owning Him as the God who seeth and knoweth all sin, however deeply hidden? It was in the language of sorrow, not of anger, that Joshua adjured him. It wrung from Achan a full admission of his crime. How miserable the whole thing must have sounded in his own ears, when he had put the facts of his sin into naked words; how paltry the price at which he had sold himself, when it was brought into the broad sunlight and "laid out before the Lord," in the sight of Joshua and of all Israel. One thing more only remained to be done. They

[1] We infer that the guilty tribe, kindred, family, and individual household (being the four divisions according to which all Israel was arranged) was designated by the *lot*, from the fact that the expression rendered "*taken*" in Josh. vii. is exactly the same as that word in 1 Sam. x. 20, and xiv. 41, 42. Again, the expressions "the lot came up" (Josh. xviii. 11) or "came forth" (xix. 1), seems to indicate that the lot was drawn—probably out of an urn—in the manner described in the text.

led forth the wretched man, with all his household, and all that belonged to them, and all Israel stoned him.[1] And then they burned the dead body,[2] and buried all beneath a heap of stones, alike as a memorial and a warning. But the valley they called that of "Achor," or *trouble*—while the echoes of that story sounded through Israel's history to latest times, in woe and in weal, for judgment and for hope (Is. lxv. 10; Hos. ii. 15).

The sin of Israel having been removed, God once more assured Joshua of His presence to give success to the undertaking against Ai. In pledge thereof He was even pleased to indicate the exact means which were to be used in reducing the city. A corps of 30,000 men was accordingly detailed, of whom 5000 were placed in ambush on the west side of Ai,[3] where, under shelter of the wood, their presence was concealed from Ai, and, by the intervening hill, from Bethel. While the main body of the Israelites under Joshua were to draw away the defenders of Ai by feigned flight, this corps was at a given signal to take the city, and after having set it on fire, to turn against the retreating men. Such was the plan of attack,

[1] Most commentators read Josh. vii. 24, 25, as implying that the sons and daughters of Achan were stoned with him, supposing that his family could not have been ignorant of their father's sin. Of the latter there is, however, no indication in the text. It will also be noticed that in ver. 25 the *singular* number is used: "All Israel stoned him;" "and they raised over him a great heap of stones." In that case, the plural number which follows ("and burned them," etc.) would refer only to the oxen, asses, and sheep, and to all that Achan possessed.

[2] This was an aggravation of the ordinary punishment of death, Lev. xx. 14. We may here also explain that the expression "wrought folly in Israel" (Josh. vii. 15), refers to that which is opposed to the character and dignity of God's people, as in Gen. xxxiv. 7.

[3] Interpreters have found considerable difficulties in Josh. viii. 3, as compared with vers. 10-12, and accordingly suggested, that as the two letters ח and ל—the one indicating the number five, the other thirty—are very like each other, there may have been a mistake in copying ver. 3, where it should read 5000 instead of 30,000. But there really is no need for resorting to this theory, and I believe that the narrative, fairly read, conveys the meaning expressed by me in the text.

and it was closely adhered to. "The ambush" lay on the west of Ai, while the main body of the host pitched north of the city, a valley intervening between them and Ai. Next, Joshua moved into the middle of that valley. Early the following morning the king of Ai discovered this advance of the Israelitish camp, and moved with his army to the "appointed place,"[1] right in front of "the plain," which, as we know from the description of travellers, was covered by olive trees. The battlefield was well chosen, since Ai occupied the vantage-ground on the slope, while an advance by Israel would be checked and broken by the olive plantation which they would have to traverse. Joshua and all Israel now feigned a retreat, and fled in an easterly direction towards the wilderness. Upon this, all the people that were in Ai, in their eager haste to make the victory decisive, " allowed themselves to be called away "[2] to pursue after Israel, till they were drawn a considerable distance from the city. The olive plantation now afforded those who had lain in ambush shelter for their advance. The preconcerted signal was given. Joshua, who probably occupied a height apart, watching the fight, lifted his spear. As the outposts of the ambush saw it, and reported that the signal for their advance had been given, a rush would be made up the steep sides of the hill towards the city. But the signal would also be perceived and understood by the main army of Israel, and they now anxiously watched the result of movements which they could not follow. They had not long to wait. Above the dark green olive trees, above the rising slopes, above the white walls, curled slowly in the clear morning air the smoke of the burning city. Something in the attitude and movements of Israel must have betrayed it, for " the men of Ai looked behind them," only to see that all was lost, and no means of escape left them. And now the host of Israel "turned again," while those who had

---

[1] Not "time," as in our Authorised Version, which would give no meaning.
[2] This is the real meaning of the form of the Hebrew verb, and makes the narrative most pictorial.

set Ai on fire advanced in an opposite direction. Between these two forces the men of Ai were literally crushed. Not one of them escaped from that bloody plain and slope. The slaughter extended to the district around. Finally, the king of Ai was put to death, and his dead body "hanged upon a tree till eventide."[1] But of what had been Ai "they made a *Tel* (or heap) for ever." Never was Scripture saying more literally fulfilled than this. For a long time did modern explorers in vain seek for the site of Ai, where they knew it must have stood. "The inhabitants of the neighbouring villages," writes Canon Williams, to whom the merit of the identification really belongs, "declared repeatedly and emphatically that this was *Tel*, and nothing else. I was satisfied that it should be so when, on subsequent reference to the original text of Josh. viii. 28, I found it written, that 'Joshua burnt Ai, and made it a *Tel* for ever, even a desolation unto this day!' There are many *Tels* in modern Palestine, that land of *Tels*, each *Tel* with some other name attached to it to mark the former site. But the site of Ai has no other name 'unto this day.' It is simply *et-Tel—the heap* 'par excellence.'"

[1] It does not appear that "hanging" was one of the modes of execution under the Mosaic Law. From Deut. xxi. 22, we learn that in certain cases the criminal was put to death, and *after that* his dead body hung on a tree till eventide. This is fully confirmed by Josh. x. 26. The Rabbinical Law (Sanh. vii. 3 ; xi. 1) recognises strangulation, but not hanging, as a mode of execution in the lightest cases to which the punishment of death attached. Full details are given as to the manner in which the punishment was to be administered.

CHAPTER IX.

Solemn Dedication of the Land and of Israel on Mounts Ebal and Gerizim—The Deceit of the Gibeonites.

(JOSH. VIII. 30. IX.)

BY the miraculous fall of Jericho God had, so to speak, given to His people the key to the whole land; with the conquest of Ai they had themselves entered, in His strength, upon possession of it. The first and most obvious duty now was, to declare, by a grand national act, in what character Israel meant to hold what it had received of God. For, as previously explained, it could never have been the Divine object in all that had been, or would be done, merely to substitute one nation for another in the possession of Palestine, but rather to destroy the heathen, and to place in their room His own redeemed and sanctified people, so that on the ruins of the hostile kingdom of this world, His own might be established. To mark the significance of the act by which Israel was to declare this, it had before been prescribed by Moses as a first duty (Deut. xxvii. 2), and detailed directions given for it (Deut. xxvii.). The act itself was to consist of *three parts*. The law—that is, the commands, "statutes," and "rights," contained in the Pentateuch—was to be written on "great stones," previously covered with "plaster," in the manner in which inscriptions were made on the monuments of Egypt.[1] Then sacrifices were to be offered on an altar of "whole stones." The memorial stones were to be set up, and

---

[1] In the drier climate of Palestine such inscriptions would of course last much longer than in our own country. Still, they could not have been so durable as if *graven* on these stones. May it not be, that this "profession" was intended for that, rather than for all future generations? For, though

the sacrifices offered on Mount Ebal. But the third was to be the most solemn part of the service. The priests[1] with the Ark were to occupy the intermediate valley, and six of the tribes (Simeon, Levi, Judah, Issachar, Joseph, and Benjamin)—those which had sprung from the lawful wives of Israel—were to stand on Mount Gerizim, while the other six (of whom five had sprung from Leah's and Rachel's maids, Reuben being added to them on account of his great sin, Gen. xlix. 4) were placed on Mount Ebal. Then, as the priests in the valley beneath read the words of blessing, the tribes on Mount Gerizim were to respond by an *Amen;* and as they read the words of the curses, those on Mount Ebal were similarly to give their solemn assent —thus expressly taking upon themselves each obligation, with its blessing in the observance, and its curse in the breach thereof. An historical parallel here immediately recurs to our minds. As, on his first entrance into Canaan, Abraham had formally owned Jehovah by rearing an altar unto Him (Gen. xii. 7), and as Jacob had, on his return, paid the vow which he had recorded at Bethel (Gen. xxxv. 7), so Israel now consecrated its possession of the land by receiving it as from the Lord, by recording His name, and by taking upon itself all the obligations of the covenant.

A glance at the map will enable us to realise the scene. From Ai and Bethel the direct route northwards leads by Shiloh to Shechem (Judges xxi. 19). The journey would occupy altogether about eleven hours. Of course, Israel could not have realised at the time that they were just then travelling along what would become the great highway from Galilee to Jerusalem, so memorable in after-history. Leaving the sanctuary of Shiloh a little aside, they would climb a rocky ridge. Before them a noble prospect spread. This was the

---

it was indeed binding upon all succeeding generations—as the record of the transaction in Scripture shows—yet each generation must take up for itself the profession to be the Lord's.

[1] That this devolved not upon the Levites generally, but specially upon the priests, appears from Josh. viii. 33.

future rich portion of Ephraim: valleys covered with corn, hills terraced to their tops, the slopes covered with vines and olive-yards. Onwards the host moved, till it reached a valley, bounded south and north by mountains, which run from west to east. This was the exact spot on which Abram had built his first altar (Gen. xii. 7); here, also, had Jacob's first settlement been (Gen. xxxiii. 19). Not a foe molested Israel on their march right up the middle of the land, partly, as previously explained, from the division of the land under so many petty chieftains, but chiefly because God had a favour unto them and to the work to which they had set their hands. Travellers speak in rapturous terms of the beauty of the valley of Shechem, even in the present desolateness of the country. It is a pass which intersects the mountain-chain, that runs through Palestine from south to north. To the south it is bounded by the range of Gerizim, to the north by that of Ebal. From where the priests with the Ark took up their position on the gentle rise of the valley, both Gerizim and Ebal appear hollowed out, forming, as it were, an amphitheatre,[1] while "the limestone strata, running up in a succession of ledges to the top of the hills, have all the appearance of benches." Here, occupying every available inch of ground, were crowded the tribes of Israel: men, women, and children, "as well the strangers, and he that was born among them." As they stood close together, the humblest in Israel by the side of the "officers," "elders," and "judges," all eagerly watching what passed in the valley, or solemnly responding to blessing or curse, a scene was enacted, the like of which had not before been witnessed upon earth, and which could never fade from the memory.[2]

[1] This peculiarity was noticed by Canon Williams, and also specially referred to by Capt. Wilson, R.E., from whom the quotation within inverted commas is made.

[2] *All* travellers are agreed on two points: 1. That there could be no difficulty whatever in distinctly hearing both from Ebal and Gerizim anything that was spoken in the valley. 2. That these two mountains afforded sufficient standing-ground for all Israel. We note these two points in answer to possible objections Happily in the present instance we have

It is noteworthy that, on Mount Ebal, whence came the responses to the curses, the great stones were set up on which "the law" was written, and that there also the sacrifices were offered. This is in itself characteristic. Perhaps even the circumstance is not without significance, that they who stood on Mount Ebal must have had their view *bounded* by the mountains of Benjamin. Not so they who occupied Gerizim, the mount whence came the responses to the blessings. For the view which greeted those who at early morn crowded the top of the Mount of Blessings, was only second to that vouchsafed to Moses from the summit of Pisgah. If less in extent than the latter, it was more distinct and detailed.[1] All Central Palestine lay spread like a map before the wondering gaze of Israel. Tabor, Gilboa, the hills of Galilee rose in succession; in the far-distance snow-capped Hermon bounded the horizon, with sweet valleys and rich fields intervening. Turning to the right, they would descry the Lake of Galilee, and follow the cleft of the Jordan valley, marking beyond it Bashan, Ajalon, Gilead, and even Moab; to their left, the Mediterranean from Carmel to Gaza was full in view, the blue outline far away dimly suggesting thoughts of the "isles of the Gentiles," and the blessings in store for them. Far as the eye could reach—and beyond it, to the uttermost bounds of the earth—would the scene which they witnessed in that valley below be repeated; the echo of the blessings to which they responded on that mount would resound, till, having wakened every valley, it would finally be sent back in songs of praise and thanksgiving from a redeemed earth. And so did Israel on that spring morning consecrate Palestine unto the LORD, taking sea and lake, mountain and valley—the most hallowed spots in their history—as witnesses of their covenant.

From this solemn transaction the Israelites moved, as we

---

express and independent testimony to put such cavils out of court. According to Dr. Thomson (*The Land and the Book*, i. p. 203), the valley is about sixty rods wide.

[1] Comp. Canon Tristram's *Land of Israel*, p. 153.

gather from Josh. ix. 6, to Gilgal, where they seem to have formed a permanent camp. The mention of this place in Deut. xi. 30, where it is described as "beside the oaks of Moreh,"[1] that is, near the spot of Abram's first altar (Gen. xii. 7), implies a locality well-known at the time, and, as we might almost conjecture from its after history, a sort of traditional sanctuary. This alone would suffice to distinguish this Gilgal from the first encampment of Israel east of Jericho, which only obtained its name from the event which there occurred. Besides, it is impossible to suppose that Joshua marched back from Shechem to the banks of Jordan (ix. 6; x. 6, 7, 9, 15, 43), and, again, that he did so a second time, after the battles in Galilee, to make apportionment of the land among the people by the banks of Jordan (xiv. 6). Further, the localisation of Gilgal near the banks of Jordan would be entirely incompatible with what we know of the after-history of that place. Gilgal was one of the three cities where Samuel judged the people (1 Sam. vii. 16); here, also, he offered sacrifices, when the Ark was no longer in the tabernacle at Shiloh (1 Sam. x. 8; xiii. 7-9; xv. 21); and there, as in a central sanctuary, did all Israel gather to renew their allegiance to Saul (1 Sam. xi. 14). Later on, Gilgal was the great scene of Elisha's ministry (2 Kings ii. 1), and still later it became a centre of idolatrous worship (Hos. iv. 15; ix. 15; xii. 11; Amos iv. 4; v. 5). All these considerations lead to the conclusion, that the Gilgal which formed the site of Joshua's encampment is the modern *Jiljilieh*, a few miles from Shiloh, and about the same distance from Bethel—nearly equi-distant from Shechem and from Jerusalem.[2]

In this camp at Gilgal a strange deputation soon arrived. Professedly, and apparently, the travellers had come a long distance. For their garments were worn, their sandals clouted, their provisions dry and mouldy,[3] and the skins in which their

---

[1] This is the correct rendering.
[2] Comp. Robinson's *Biblical Researches*, vol. ii. p. 243.
[3] Literally, "dotted over."

wine had been were rent and "bound up" (like purses), as in the East wine-bottles of goat's skin are temporarily repaired on a long journey. According to their own account, they lived far beyond the boundaries of Palestine, where their fellow-townsmen had heard what the Lord had done in Egypt, and again to Sihon and to Og, wisely omitting from the catalogue the miraculous passage of Jordan and the fall of Jericho, as of too recent date for their theory. Attracted by the name of Jehovah, Israel's God, who had done such wonders, they had been sent to make "a league" with Israel. It must have been felt that the story did not sound probable—at least, to any who had learned to realise the essential enmity of heathenism against the kingdom of God, and who understood that so great a change as the report of these men implied could not be brought about by "the hearing of the ear." Besides, what they proposed was not to make submission to, but a league with, Israel; by which not merely life, but their land and liberty, would be secured to them.[1] But against any *league* with the inhabitants of Canaan, Israel had been specially warned (Ex. xxiii. 32; xxxiv. 12; Numb. xxxiii. 55; Deut. vii. 2). What if, after all, they were neighbours? The suspicion seems to have crossed the minds of Joshua and of the elders, and even to have been expressed by them, only to be set aside by the protestations of the pretended ambassadors. It was certainly a mark of religious superficiality and self-confidence on the part of the elders of Israel to have consented on such grounds to "a league." The sacred text significantly puts it: "And the men (the elders of Israel) took of their victuals (according to the common Eastern fashion of eating bread and salt with a guest who is received as a friend), but they asked not counsel at the mouth of Jehovah."

Their mistake soon became apparent. Three days later, and Israel found that the pretended foreigners were in reality neighbours! Meanwhile, the kings or chieftains who ruled in Western Palestine had been concerting against Israel a

---

[1] In Josh. ix. 15, we read indeed: "Joshua . . . made a league with them, to let them live."

combined movement of their forces from "the hills," or highlands of Central Palestine, from "the valleys," or the *Shephelah* (low country), between the mountain-chain and the sea, and "from the coasts of the great sea over against Lebanon," that is, from Joppa northwards by the sea-shore. The existence of the small confederate republic of Gibeon with its three associate cities in the midst of small monarchies throws a curious light upon the state of Palestine at the time; and the jealousy which would naturally exist between them helps to explain alike the policy of the Gibeonites, and the revenge which the Canaanitish kings were shortly afterwards preparing to take. The history of the republic of Gibeon is interesting. "Gibeon was a great city, as one of the royal cities .... greater than Ai, and all the men thereof were mighty" (Josh. x. 2). Its inhabitants were "Hivites" (xi. 19). Afterwards Gibeon fell to the lot of Benjamin, and became a priest-city (xviii. 25; xxi. 17). When Nob was destroyed by Saul, the tabernacle was transported to Gibeon, where it remained till the temple was built by Solomon (1 Chron. xvi. 39; xxi. 29; 1 Kings iii. 4; 2 Chron. i. 3).[1] It lay about two hours to the north-west of Jerusalem, and is represented by the modern village of *el-Jib*. Its three associate towns were *Chephirah*, about three hours' west from Gibeon, the modern *Kefir*; *Beeroth*, about ten miles north of Jerusalem, the modern *el-Bireh*—both cities afterwards within the possession of Benjamin; and *Kirjath-Jearim*, "the city of groves," probably

[1] The following historical notice in the *Mishnah* is so interesting, that we give its translation: "When they went to Gilgal, high places were allowed (for ordinary worship); the most holy offerings were eaten 'within,' between the veils; the less holy ones in every place. When they went to Shiloh, the high places were forbidden. There were not there beams (for the house of God), but a building of stones below (a kind of foundation) and the curtains (tabernacle) above, and that was (in Scripture-language) 'rest.' Then the most holy offerings were eaten 'within,' between the veils, and the less holy and the second tithe anywhere within sight (of Shiloh). When they went to Nob and to Gibeon, high places were allowed. Then the most holy offerings were eaten 'within,' between the veils, and the less holy ones in all the cities of Israel" (Sevachim xiv. 5, 6, 7).

so called from its olive, fig, and other plantations, as its modern representative, *Kuriet-el-Enab*, is from its vineyards. The latter city, which was afterwards allotted to Judah, is about three hours from Jerusalem; and there the Ark remained from the time of its return from the Philistines to that of David (1 Sam. vii. 2; 2 Sam. vi. 2; 1 Chron. xiii. 5, 6).

When the people learned the deceit practised upon them, they "murmured against the princes;" but the latter refused to break their solemn oath, so far as it insured the lives and safety of the Gibeonites. If they had sworn rashly and presumptuously "by Jehovah, God of Israel," it would have only added another and a far more grievous sin to have broken their oath; not to speak of the effect upon the heathen around. The principle applying to this, as to similar rash undertakings, is, that a solemn obligation, however incurred, must be considered binding, *unless its observance involve fresh sin*.[1] But in this instance it manifestly did *not* involve fresh sin. For the main reason of the destruction of the Canaanites was their essential hostility to the kingdom of God. The danger to Israel, accruing from this, could be avoided in a solitary instance. With a view to this, the Gibeonites were indeed spared, but attached as "bondmen" to the sanctuary, where they and their descendants performed all menial services[2] (Josh. ix. 23). Nor, as the event proved, did they ever betray their trust, or lead Israel into idolatry.[3] Still, as a German writer observes, the rashness of Israel's princes, and the conduct of the Gibeonites, conveys to the church at all times solemn warning against the devices and the deceit of the world, which, when outward advantage offers, seeks a friendly alliance with, or even reception into, the visible kingdom of God.

---

[1] As for example in the case of monastic vows.

[2] From the concluding words of Josh. ix. 27, it has been rightly inferred that the Book of Joshua must date from a period previous to the building of the temple by Solomon.

[3] From 2 Sam. xxi. 1, we gather that, in his carnal zeal, Saul had broken the oath of the princes—with what result appears from the narrative.

CHAPTER X.

The Battle of Gibeon—Conquest of the South of Canaan—The Battle of Merom—Conquest of the North of Canaan—State of the land at the close of the seven years' war.

(JOSH. X.-XII.)

THE surrender of Gibeon would fill the kings of Southern Canaan with dismay. It was, so to speak, treason within their own camp; it gave Israel a strong position in the heart of the country and within easy reach of Jerusalem; while the possession of the passes leading from Gibeon would throw the whole south of Canaan open to their incursion. In the circumstances it was natural that the chieftains of the south would combine, in the first place, for the retaking of Gibeon. The confederacy, which was under the leadership of *Adoni-Zedek*,[1] king of Jerusalem,[2] embraced *Hoham*,[3] king of Hebron (about seven hours' south of Jerusalem); *Piram*,[4] king of Jarmuth, the present *Jarmuk*, about three hours' to the south-west of Jerusalem; *Japhia*,[5] king of Lachish, and *Debir*,[6] king of Eglon, both cities close to each other, and not far from Gaza, to the south-west of Hebron. The march of the combined kings was evidently rapid, and the danger pressing, for it seems to have found the Gibeonites wholly unprepared,

---

[1] The reader will notice the significant change from Melchi-Zedek, "My King righteousness," to Adoni-Zedek, "My Lord righteousness," marking the change of dynasties. See *History of the Patriarchs*, p. 86.

[2] Jerusalem, either the *habitation of peace*, or the *possession of peace*—perhaps originally the *habitation of Shalem*.

[3] *Hoham*: "the Jehovah of the multitude."

[4] *Piram*: "coursing about," wild and free.

[5] *Japhia*: exalted.   [6] *Debir*: scribe.

and their entreaty to Joshua for immediate succour was of the most urgent kind. That very night Joshua marched to their relief with "all the people of war, that is, the mighty men of valour."[1] The relieving army came upon the enemy as "suddenly" as they had appeared in sight of Gibeon. It was probably very early in the morning when Joshua and his warriors surprised the allied camp. Gibeon lay in the east, surrounded, as in a semicircle, north, west, and south, by its three confederate cities. The five kings had pushed forward within that semicircle, and camped in the "open ground at the foot of the heights of Gibeon." Animated by the assurance which God had expressly given Joshua: "Fear them not: for I have delivered them into thine hand; there shall not a man of them stand before thee," the host of Israel fell upon them with an irresistible rush. The Canaanites made but a short stand before their unexpected assailants; then fled in wild confusion towards the pass of Upper Beth-horon, "the house of caves." They gained the height before their pursuers, and were hurrying down the pass of the Nether Beth-horon, when a fearful hailstorm, such as not unfrequently sweeps over the hills of Palestine, burst upon them. It was in reality "the Lord" who, once more miraculously employing natural agency, "cast down great stones from heaven upon them;" "and they were more which died from the hailstones than they whom the children of Israel slew with the sword."[2] It was but noon; far behind Israel in the heaven stood the sun over Gibeon, and before them over Ajalon in the west hung the crescent moon. The tempest was extinguishing day and light, and the work was but half done. In the pass to Nether Beth-horon Israel might be readily divided; at any rate, the enemy might escape before their crushing defeat had assured safety to Gibeon, and given the south of Palestine to Israel. Now, or never, was the time

---

[1] We have so rendered the Hebrew particle "and" which is here used explanatively.

[2] A German writer has noticed that a similar hailstorm determined the battle of Solferino against the Austrians in 1859.

to pursue the advantage. Oh, that the sun would once more burst forth in his brightness; oh, that the all too short day were protracted "until the people had avenged themselves upon their enemies!" Then it was that Joshua burst into that impassioned prayer of faith, which is quoted in the sacred text from the "Book of Jasher,"—or "Book of the Pious,"—apparently, as we infer from 2 Sam. i. 18, a collection of poetical pieces, connected with the sublimest scenes in the history of the heroes of the kingdom of God. In this instance the quotation begins, as we take it, Josh. x. 12, and ends with ver. 15. This is proved by the insertion in ver. 15 of a notice, which in the historical narrative occurs only in ver. 43. For it is evident that Joshua did *not* return to Gilgal immediately after the battle of Gibeon (ver. 21), but pursued the war, as described in the rest of ch. x., till the whole south of Palestine was reduced. Thus verses 12-15 are a quotation from "the Book of the Pious," inserted within the Book of Joshua, the narrative of which is resumed in ver. 16. The quotation reads as follows:

"Then spake Joshua to Jehovah,
In the day Jehovah gave the Amorite before the sons of Israel,
And he spake in the sight of Israel:
Sun, on Gibeon rest still,[1]
And moon, on the valley of Ajalon!
And still rested the sun,
And the moon stood,
Till the people were avenged on their foes.

(Is not this written in the 'Book of the Pious?')

And the sun stood in mid-heaven,
And hasted not to go—like (as on) a complete day.[2]

---

[1] The word probably means "to become dumb." Accordingly, a recent Italian writer has regarded it as a poetical expression for "ceasing to shine," and treated the event as an eclipse of the sun. But the context shows that this view is untenable, and that "to become dumb" means here to rest silent or stand still.

[2] That is, like any ordinary complete day. We attach considerable importance to our rendering as here proposed.

And there was not like that day, before or after,
That Jehovah hearkened to the voice of man—
For Jehovah warred for Israel!

And Joshua returned, and all Israel with him to the camp, to Gilgal."[1]

And God hearkened to the voice of Joshua. Once more the sun burst forth, and the daylight was miraculously protracted till Israel was avenged of its enemies. Onwards rolled the tide of fugitives, hotly pursued by Israel, through the pass of Nether Beth-horon to Azekah, and thence to Makkedah.[2] Here tidings were brought to Joshua, that the five kings had hid themselves in one of the caves with which that district abounds. But Joshua would not be diverted from his object. He ordered large stones to be rolled to the mouth of the cave, and its entrance to be guarded by armed men, while the rest of the army followed the enemy and smote their "rearguard." Only broken remnants of the fugitives found shelter in the "fenced cities." Joshua himself had camped before the city of Makkedah. Thither the pursuing corps returned, and thence the war was afterwards carried on (x. 21, 29). On the morning after the victory, the five confederate kings were brought from their hiding-place. In a manner not uncommon in ancient times,[3] Joshua made his

---

[1] It is impossible here to enter on a detailed criticism. Substantially our view is that of all the best critics, except that some regard the five lines after the parenthesis as the remarks of him who inserted in the Book of Joshua the quotation from the Book of Jasher. But the poetical terms used in these five last lines render this view, to say the least of it, *most* improbable. Poetical expressions, similar to those used in the text, will recur to the reader, specially Judges v. 20: "the stars fought out of their courses (not "*in* their courses," as in Authorised Version) against Sisera." See also Ps. xviii. 10; xxix. 6; cxiv. 4-6; Isa. xxxiv. 3; lv. 12; lxiv. 1; Amos ix. 13; Mic. i. 4. The passage Hab. iii. 11 does not refer to the event in the text, as its correct rendering is: "The sun and moon enter into their habitation," that is, go into shadow. Our view does not, of course, militate against a miraculous intervention on the part of God.

[2] The locality of these two places has not been ascertained.

[3] It seems even to have been practised by the Byzantine emperors long after the Christian era. See the reference given, *Bynaeus* in Kid's *Commentary*, p. 81.

captains put their feet upon the necks of the prostrate kings, who had so lately gone forth boastfully in all the pride and pomp of war. But the lesson which Israel was to learn from their victory was not one of self-confidence in their supposed superiority, but of acknowledgment of God and confidence in Him: "Fear not, nor be dismayed, be strong and of good courage: for thus shall Jehovah do to all your enemies against whom ye fight."

The death of these five kings proved only the beginning of a campaign which may have lasted weeks, or even months, for we find that successors of these five kings afterwards shared their fate. In the end, the whole south of Canaan was in the hands of Israel, though some of the cities taken appear to have been afterwards again wrested from them, and occupied by the Canaanites.[1] The extent of the conquest is indicated (x. 41) by a line drawn south and north, westwards—"from Kadesh-barnea even unto Gaza"—and eastwards, "from the district of Goshen[2] unto Gibeon."

The campaign thus finished in the south had soon to be renewed in the north of Canaan. The means, the help, and the result were the same as before. Only, as the danger was much greater, from the multitude of Israel's opponents—"even as the sand that is upon the sea-shore,"—and from their formidable mode of warfare ("horses and chariots very many"), hitherto unknown to Israel, the Lord once more gave express assurance of victory: "I will deliver them up all slain before Israel." At the same time He enjoined "to hough (or hamstring) their horses, and burn their chariots with fire," lest Israel should be tempted to place in future their trust in such weapons. The allied forces of the northern enemy were under

---
[1] Such as Gezer (x. 33), Hebron, and Debir (xiv. 12; xv. 13-17; comp. Judges i. 10-15). Masius rightly observes, that in this expedition Joshua had rather rapidly swept over the south of Palestine than permanently and wholly occupied the country.

[2] Of course not the province of that name in Egypt, but a district in the south of Judah, probably deriving its name from the town of that name (xv. 51).

the leadership of Jabin,[1] king of Hazor,[2] which "beforetimes was the head of all those kingdoms." They consisted not only of the three neighbouring "kings" (or chieftains) of Madon, Shimron, and Achshaph,[3] but of all the kings "in the north and (on the mountain" (of Naphtali, Josh. xx. 7), of those in the Arabah, south of the Lake of Gennesaret, of those "in the plains," or valleys that stretched to the Mediterranean, and in "the heights of Dor," at the foot of Mount Carmel—in short, of all the Canaanite tribes from the Mediterranean in the south-west up to Mizpeh[4] "the view") under Mount Hermon in the far north-east.

With the rapidity and suddenness which characterised all his movements, Joshua fell upon the allied camp by the Lake Merom (the modern *el-Huleh*), and utterly routed the ill-welded mass of the enemy. The fugitive Canaanites seem to have divided into three parts, one taking the road north-west to "Zidon the Great," another that west and south-west to the "smelting-pits by the waters" (Misrephoth-Maim), and the third that to the east leading to the valley of Mizpeh. In each direction they were hotly pursued by the Israelites. One by one all their cities were taken. Those in the valleys were burnt, but those on the heights, with the exception of Hazor, left standing, as requiring only small garrisons for their occupation. Altogether the war in the south and north must have occupied at least seven years,[5] at the end of which the whole country was

---

[1] *Jabin* seems to have been the title of the kings of Hazor (Judges iv. 2).

[2] Hazor in the mountains, north of Lake Merom, was afterwards rebuilt, and again became the seat of royalty (Judges iv. 2; 1 Sam. xii. 9). Thence Sisera issued against Israel.

[3] The locality of these three places has not been ascertained; but they seem to have been in the neighbourhood of Hazor.

[4] There were several places throughout the land bearing the name of "Mizpeh" or "view." This Mizpeh was probably the modern village *Mutulleh*, which also means "prospect," situated on a hill two hundred feet high, north of Lake Merom, whence there is a splendid view.

[5] This we gather from Josh. xiv. 10. From it we learn that forty-five years had elapsed since the spies returned to Kadesh. But as thirty-eight of these were spent in the wanderings in the wilderness, it follows that the wars for the occupation of Canaan must have lasted seven years.

in the possession of Israel, from the "smooth mountain (Mount Halak) that goeth up to Seir,"—that is, the white chalk mountains in the chain of the Azazimeh, in the Negeb—as far north as "Baal-gad," the town dedicated to "Baal" as god of "fortune," the Cæsarea Philippi of the Gospels (xi. 16–18). More than that, Joshua also drove the Anakim, who had inspired the spies with such dread, from their original seats in the mountains,[1] and in and around Hebron, Debir, and Anab into the Philistine cities of Gaza, Gath, and Ashdod. From ch. xv. 14 we infer that they shortly afterwards returned, but were conquered by that veteran hero, Caleb.

To sum up all, we find that the wars under Joshua put Israel into possession of Canaan and broke the power of its inhabitants, but that the latter were not exterminated, nor yet all their cities taken by Israel (xiii. 1–6; xvii. 14, etc.; xviii. 3; xxiii. 5, 12). Indeed, such a result could scarcely have been desirable, either in reference to the country or to Israel, while, from Ex. xxiii. 28–30 and Deut vii. 22, we know that from the beginning it had not been the Divine purpose. But there was also a higher object in this. It would teach that a conquest, begun in the power of God and in believing dependence on Him, must be completed and consolidated in the same spirit. Only thus could Israel prosper as a nation. Canaan had been given to Israel by God, and given to their faith. But much was left to be done which only the same faith could achieve.

---

[1] In Josh. xi. 21 a distinction is made between "the mountains of Judah" and "the mountains of Israel." This, strange as it may sound, affords one of the undesigned evidences of the early composition of the Book of Joshua. "When Judah entered on his possession," observes a German critic, "all the other tribes were still in Gilgal (xiv. 6; xv. 1). Afterwards, when Ephraim and Manasseh entered on theirs, all Israel, except Judah, were camped in Shiloh (xvi. 1; xviii. 1), these two possessions being separated by the still unallotted territory which later was given to Benjamin (xviii. 11). What more natural than that 'the mountain' given to the 'children of Judah' should have been called 'the mountain of Judah,' and that where all the rest of Israel camped, 'the mountain of Israel,' and also 'the mountain of Ephraim' (xix. 50; xx. 7), because it was afterwards given to that tribe?"

Any conformity to the heathen around, or tolerance of heathenism, any decay of the spirit in which they had entered the land, would result not only in weakness, but in the triumph of the enemy. And so it was intended of the Lord. The lesson of all this is obvious and important. To us also has our Joshua given entrance into Canaan, and victory over our enemies—the world, the flesh, and the devil. We have *present* possession of the land. But we do not yet hold all its cities, nor are our enemies exterminated. It needs on our part constant faith; there must be no compromise with the enemy, no tolerance of his spirit, no cessation of our warfare. Only that which at first gave us the land can complete and consolidate our possession of it.

CHAPTER XI.

Distribution of the land—Unconquered districts—Tribes east of the Jordan—"The lot"—Tribes west of the Jordan—The inheritance of Caleb—Dissatisfaction of the sons of Joseph—The Tabernacle at Shiloh—Final division of the land.

(JOSH. XIII.–XXI.)

THE continuance of unsubdued races and districts soon became a source of danger, although in a direction different from what might have been anticipated. Sufficient had been gained by a series of brilliant victories to render the general tenure of the land safe to Israel. The Canaanites and other races were driven to their fastnesses, where for the time they remained on the defensive. On the other hand, a nation like Israel, accustomed to the nomadic habits of the wilderness, would scarcely feel the need of a fixed tenure of land, and readily grow weary of a desultory warfare in which each tribe had separately to make good its boundaries. Thus it came that Joshua had grown old, probably ninety or a hundred years, while the work intrusted to him was far from completed. In the far south and along the sea-shore the whole district from the brook of Egypt[1] to Ekron was still held, in the south-west and south-east, by the Geshurites and the Avites, while the territory farther north from Ekron to Gaza was occupied by the five lords of the Philistines (Josh. xiii. 2, 3). According to the Divine direction, all these, though not descended from Canaan (Gen. x. 14), were to be "counted to the Canaanites," that is, treated as such. Travelling still farther northwards along the sea-shore, the whole "land of the Canaanites" or of the Phœnicians far up to the celebrated "cave"[2] near Sidon, and beyond it to Aphek[3] and even "to the borders of the Amorites"[4] was still unconquered. Thence eastward across Lebanon as far as Baal-gad and "the entering into Hamath,"[5] and again back from Mount Lebanon, across country, to the "smelting-pits on the waters," was subject to the Sidonians or Phœnicians.[6] Yet all this belonged by Divine gift to Israel. That it was still unoccupied by them, and that Joshua was now old, constituted the ground for the Divine command to make immediate distribution of the land among the tribes. It was as if, looking to His promise, God would have bidden Israel consider the whole land as theirs, and simply

---

[1] Literally: "from Shichor, in the face of Egypt," or rather "from the black (river) to the east of Egypt." This was the brook *Rhinocorura*, the modern *el-Arish*.

[2] Left untranslated (*Mearah*) in the Authorised Version. The cave, which is east of Sidon, still serves as a hiding-place to the Druses.

[3] The modern *Afkah*, on a terrace of Mount Lebanon, by the principal source of the river Adonis, in a lovely situation.

[4] The explanation of this is doubtful. Possibly it means: as far east as the territory of Og, king of Bashan, which formerly belonged to the Amorites.

[5] *Hamath*, a district in Syria, with a capital of the same name on the Orontes.

[6] The particle "*and*," put in *italics* in our Authorised Version, is not in the text of Josh. xiii. 6. The clause, "all the Sidonians" is explanatory, not additional.

go forward, in faith of that promise and in obedience to His command.[1]

It will be remembered that only nine and a half tribes remained to be provided for, since "unto the tribe of Levi He gave none inheritance," other than what came from the sanctuary, while Reuben, Gad, and half Manasseh had had their portions assigned by Moses east of the Jordan.[2] That territory was bounded by Moab along the *south-eastern* shores of the Dead Sea, while the *eastern* border of Reuben and Gad was held by Ammon. Both these nations were by Divine command not to be molested by Israel (Deut. ii. 9, 19). The southernmost and smallest portion of the district east of the Jordan belonged to Reuben. His territory extended from the river Arnon, in the south, to where Jordan flowed into the Dead Sea, and embraced the original kingdom of Sihon. Northward of it, the Ammonites had once held possession, but had been driven out by Sihon. That new portion of Sihon's kingdom was given not to Reuben but to Gad. The territory of that tribe ran along the Jordan as far as the Lake of Gennesaret—the upper portion (from Mahanaim) narrowing almost into a point. North of this was the possession of the half tribe of Manasseh, which embraced the whole of Bashan. It occupied by far the largest extent of area. But from its position it also lay most open to constant nomadic incursions, and possessed comparatively few settled cities.

The division of the land among the nine and a half tribes[3] was, in strict accordance with Divine direction (Numb. xxvi. 52-56; xxxiii. 54; xxxiv. 2-29), made by Eleazar, Joshua, and one representative from each of the ten tribes. It was

---

[1] With the register of the defeated kings (Josh. xii.) the first part of the Book of Joshua ends, and Part II. begins with ch. xiii.

[2] Although geographical details may seem dry to some, they are most important for the proper understanding of the Bible narrative. They may also be made alike interesting and spiritually useful, if the history of these places is traced in the various passages of Scripture where they are mentioned.

[3] The children of Joseph were counted two tribes.

decided by the "lot," which probably, however, only determined the *situation* of each inheritance, whether north or south, inland or by the sea-shore, not its *extent* and precise boundaries. These would depend upon the size of each tribe. In point of fact, the original arrangements had in some cases to be afterwards modified, not as to tribal localisation, which was unalterably fixed by the Divine lot, but as to extent of territory. Thus Judah had to give up part of its possession to Simeon (Josh. xix. 9), while Dan, whose portion proved too small, obtained certain cities both from Judah and from Ephraim.[1] As regards the lot, we may probably accept the Rabbinical tradition, that two urns were set out, one containing the names of the ten (or rather nine and a half) tribes, the other the designation of the various districts into which the country had been arranged, and that from each a lot was successively drawn, to designate first the tribe, and then the locality of its inheritance.

This is not the place, however interesting the task, to

[1] In connection with this we may note the curious and undesigned evidence, that we have in the text the real and original allotment of the land by Joshua himself. As so often, it is derived from an objection suggested. For there are strange divergencies in the sacred text. In describing the lots of *Judah* and of *Benjamin*, *the boundaries are accurately marked*, and a *complete list of cities* is given; in those of *Ephraim* and *half Manasseh* there is *no register of cities*; in those of *Simeon* and *Dan* only lists of cities: in those of the other tribes evidently an incomplete tracing of boundaries and lists of cities. Now when we consider the history, we conclude that this is just what we would have expected in a contemporary document. Josh. xv. xvi. assigns a definite portion to Judah; ch. xvii. to Ephraim and half Manasseh, about which, however, they complain as being partly occupied by Canaanites whom they dared not attack (ver. 16). Hence in their case there is no register of cities. On the other hand, the lot of Benjamin, being between Judah and Joseph (xviii. 11), was completely occupied, and the register is complete. The territories of Simeon and Dan have no boundary mark, only a register of cities, because they really formed part of the territories of Judah and Ephraim. Lastly, the defectiveness in the description of the other tribal lots arises from so much of the country being still in the hands of the Canaanites. It is evident that such a register could not have dated from a later period, when the tribes were in full possession, but must be the original register of Joshua.

describe the exact boundaries and cities of each tribe. We can only attempt the most general outline, which the reader must fill up for himself. Beginning in the far south, at Kadesh in the wilderness, and along the borders of Edom, we are within the territory of Simeon; north of it, bounded on the west by the land of the Philistines, and on the east by the Dead Sea, is the possession of Judah; beyond it, to the east, that of Benjamin, and to the west, that of Dan; north of Dan we reach Ephraim, and then Manasseh, the possession of Issachar running along the east of these two territories, and ending at the southern extremity of the Lake of Gennesaret; by the shore of that lake and far beyond it is the territory of Naphtali, first a narrow slip, then widening, and finally merging into a point. Asher occupied the seaboard, north of Manasseh; while, lastly, Zebulon is as it were wedged in between Issachar, Manasseh, Asher, and Naphtali.

It only remains briefly to notice the incidents recorded in connection with the territorial division of the land.

1. It seems that before the first lot was drawn in the camp at Gilgal, Caleb, the son of Jephunneh, came forward with a special claim. It will be remembered, that of the twelve princes sent from Kadesh only he and Joshua had brought "a good report of the land," in the spiritual sense of the expression, as encouraging the people to go forward. And when the Divine sentence doomed that rebellious generation to death in the wilderness, Caleb and Joshua alone were excepted. Strictly speaking, no more than this might have been implied in the promise by Moses, now claimed by Caleb: "Surely the land whereon thy feet have trodden shall be thine inheritance" (Josh. xiv. 9), since to have survived was to obtain the inheritance.[1] But there seems to have been more than merely a promise of survival, although it alone is mentioned in Numb. xiv. 24, 30. For we infer from the words and the attitude of

---

[1] Even these words (xiv. 12): "Now therefore give me this mountain, whereof Jehovah spake in that day;" do not necessarily imply that that "mountain" was actually assigned to Caleb on "that day."

Caleb, and from the similar privileges afterwards accorded to Joshua (xix. 49, 50), that Moses had, by direction of the Lord, given these two a right of special and personal choice. This on account of their exceptional faithfulness, and as the sole survivors of the generation to whom the land had been given. It was as if the surviving proprietors might choose their portion,[1] before those who, so to speak, were only next of kin had theirs allotted to them. Of this Caleb now reminds Joshua, and in words of such vigorous faith, as make us love still better the tried old warrior of Jehovah. Appearing at the head of "the house of fathers," in Judah, of which he was the head,[2] he first refers to the past, then owns God's faithfulness in having preserved him to the age of eighty-five, with strength and courage undiminished for the holy war. From xiv. 9 we infer that, when the twelve spies distributed themselves singly over the land, for the purposes of their mission, Caleb specially "searched" that "mountain," which was the favourite haunt of the dreaded Anakim. If this be so, we discover a special meaning and special faith on the part of Caleb, when he, rather than Joshua, attempted to "still the people before Moses, and said, Let us go up at once" (Numb. xiii. 30). In that case there was also special suitableness in the Divine bestowal made then and there: "Surely the land whereon thy feet have trodden shall be thine inheritance" (Josh. xiv. 9, 12). But even if otherwise, the courage and faith of the old warrior shine only the more brightly,

---

[1] It is difficult to arrive at a certain conclusion, whether at Kadesh districts were actually assigned to Caleb and to Joshua, or to Caleb alone, or whether the choice of districts was accorded to both, or to one of them. The reader will infer our conclusion from the text.

[2] "Caleb, the son of Jephunneh the Kenazite," that is, a son of Kenaz, who was a descendant of Hezron, the son of Pharez, a grandson of Judah (1 Chron. ii. 5, 18). The name "Kenaz" seems to have been rather marked in the family, as it recurs again later, 1 Chron. iv. 15. Caleb was the chieftain or head of one of "the houses of fathers" in Judah, and to the presence of this his "house"—not of the whole tribe—refer the words (Josh. xiv. 6): "Then the children of Judah came unto Joshua."

as, recalling the terror formerly inspired by the Anakim and the strength of their cities, he claims that very portion for his own. Yet his courage bears no trace of self-sufficiency,[1] only of believing dependence upon the Lord. "If so be Jehovah will be with me, and I shall drive them out" (ver. 12).

The claim thus made was immediately acknowledged, Joshua adding his blessing on Caleb's proposed undertaking. But it was some time later that the expedition was actually made,[2] when Caleb offered the hand of his daughter, Achsah, as the prize of taking the great stronghold of Debir, the ancient Kirjath-sepher, or "book-city,"—probably the fortified depository of the sacred books of the Anakim. The prize was won by a near kinsman, Othniel,[3] who, after the death of Joshua, was the first "judge" of Israel (Judges iii. 9). The history of the campaign, with its accompanying incidents, is inserted in Josh. xv. 13-19, because, both geographically and historically, it fits into that part of the description of the inheritance of Judah.[4]

2. The first signs of future weakness and disagreement appeared so early as when the lot designated the possession of the children of Joseph (Ephraim and half the tribe of Manasseh).

[1] In this sense the words must be understood (Josh. xiv. 7): "I brought word again, as it was in mine heart," that is, according to my conscientious conviction. Similarly the expression (ver. 8): "but I wholly followed the Lord," means, that his allegiance to the Lord was not shaken either by the evil report of the other spies, or by the murmuring and threatening of the people.

[2] It seems to have taken place after the death of Joshua, and is recorded in Judges i. 11, etc.

[3] It is not easy to decide whether Othniel was the son of Kenaz, who was a younger brother of Caleb, or whether he was himself Caleb's younger brother (Judges iii. 9). The punctuation of the Masorethists is in favour of the latter view, nor was the marriage of an uncle with his niece contrary to the Mosaic law.

[4] Two other critical remarks may here find a place. 1. Our present Hebrew text seems incomplete between Josh. xv. 59 and 60. Here the LXX. insert, no doubt from a more perfect MS., a list of other eleven cities, among them Bethlehem. 2. The closing notice of ver. 63 helps us to fix the date of the Book of Joshua.

Theirs was the richest and most fertile in the land, including the plain of Sharon, capable of producing almost boundless store, and of becoming the granary of the whole land. On that ground then no complaint could be made. Nor could any reasonable objection be taken to the size of their lot,[1] provided they were prepared to go forward in faith and occupy it as against the Canaanites, who still held the principal towns in the valley, all the way from Bethshean by the Jordan to the plain of Jezreel and farther. But the children of Joseph were apparently afraid of such encounter because of the iron chariots of their enemies. Equally unwilling were they to clear the wooded heights of Ephraim, which connect the range north of Samaria with Mount Carmel, and where the Perizzites and the Rephaim had their haunts. Rather did they clamour for an additional "portion" (xvii. 14). Their demands were, of course, refused; Joshua turning the boastful pride in which they had been made into an argument for action on their part against the common enemy (ver. 18).[2] But this murmuring of the children of Joseph, and the spirit from which it proceeded, gave sad indications of dangers in the near future. National disintegration, tribal jealousies, coupled with boastfulness and unwillingness to execute the work given them of God, were only too surely foreboded in the conduct of the children of Joseph.

3. If such troubles were to be averted, it was high time to seek a revival of religion. With that object in view, "the whole congregation of the children of Israel" were now

---

[1] Ephraim numbered 32,500 and half Manasseh 26,350 men capable of bearing arms (Numb. xxvi. 34, 37), or, both together, 58,850, while Judah numbered 76,500, and even Dan and Issachar respectively 64,400 and 64,300.

[2] The Authorised Version renders the last clause of ver. 18: "though they have iron chariots, and though they be strong." The true rendering is not "though," but "for." Most commentators regard this as an irony, implying that it needed such strong tribes as the sons of Joseph! But I regard it as rather a covert appeal to their faith—"just because it is so, ye shall drive them out."

gathered at *Shiloh*, and the tabernacle set up there (xviii. 1). The choice of Shiloh was, no doubt, Divinely directed (Deut. xii. 11). It was specially suitable for the purpose, not only from its central situation—about eight hours' north of Jerusalem, and five south of Shechem—but from its name, which recalled *rest*[1] and the promised rest-giver (Gen. xlix. 10). Then Joshua solemnly admonished the assembled people as to their "slackness" in taking possession of the land which Jehovah had given them. To terminate further jealousies, he asked the people to choose three representatives from each of the seven tribes whose inheritance had not yet been allotted. These were to "go through the land and describe it," that is, to make a general estimate and valuation, rather than an accurate survey, "with reference to their inheritance,"[2] that is, in view of their inheriting the land. After their return to Shiloh these twenty-one delegates were to divide the land into seven portions, when the lot would assign to each tribe the place of its inheritance.

4. The arrangement thus made was fully carried out.[3] After its completion Joshua, who, like Caleb, had received a special promise, was allowed to choose his own city within his tribal inheritance of Ephraim.[4] Finally, the cities of refuge, six in number; the Levitical cities, thirty-five in number; and the thirteen cities of the priests,[5] the sons of Aaron, were formally set aside.

---

[1] *Shiloh* means rest.   [2] So literally.

[3] According to Josephus, it took seven months; according to the Rabbis, seven years. It need scarcely be said, that both suppositions are equally void of foundation. Josephus also imagines, that there was only one deputy from each tribe—or seven in all—to whom he adds three men expert in surveying (*Ant.* v. 1, 20, 21).

[4] Considering that Joshua was himself a descendant of Joseph, his reply to the complaints of his tribe show the more clearly his uprightness and fitness for his calling.

[5] Of the six cities of refuge three were west of the Jordan: *Kadesh* (Naphtali—north), *Shechem* (Ephraim—centre), and *Hebron* (Judah—south); three east of the Jordan: *Bezer* (Reuben—south), *Ramoth* (Gad—centre), and *Golan* (Manasseh—north). The number of cities assigned to the Levites

Thus, *so far as the Lord was concerned,* He " gave unto Israel all the land which He sware to give unto their fathers; and they possessed it, and dwelt therein. And Jehovah gave them rest round about, according to all that He sware unto their fathers: and there stood not a man of all their enemies before them; Jehovah delivered all their enemies into their hand. There failed not ought of any good thing Jehovah had spoken unto the house of Israel; all came to pass" (Josh xxi. 43-45).

CHAPTER XII.

Return of the two and a half Tribes to their Homes— Building of an Altar by them—Embassy to them— Joshua's Farewell Addresses—Death of Joshua— Review of his Life and Work.

(JOSH. XXII.-XXIV.)

YET another trial awaited Joshua, ere he put off the armour and laid him down to rest. Happily, it was one which he rather dreaded than actually experienced. The work given him to do was ended, and each of the tribes had entered on its God-given inheritance. And now the time had come for those faithful men who so truly had discharged their undertaking to

---

(thirty-five) cannot be regarded as too large. The second census gave the number of male Levites at 23,000. This, with a proportionate number of females, has been calculated to give a population of about 1300 for each of the thirty-five towns. Besides, it should be remembered, that *the Levites were not the sole inhabitants of such towns.* This should also be taken into account in regard to the assignment of thirteen cities to the descendants of Aaron, although their number has been computed at the time at two hundred families. Probably this is exaggerated, even admitting that as Aaron's two sons had 24 descendants (1 Chron. xxiv.), the next generation might have numbered 144 males, and the next again (at the time of Joshua) between 800 and 900 descendants. But, irrespective of this, the law had to provide not for that period, but for all time to come.

recross Jordan, and "get unto to the land of their possession." These many years had the men of Reuben, Gad, and Manasseh fought and waited by the side of their brethren. And now that God had given them rest, Joshua dismissed the tried warriors with a blessing, only bidding them fight in their own homes that other warfare, in which victory meant loving the Lord, walking in His ways, keeping His commandments, and cleaving unto and serving Him.

It must have been with a heavy heart that Joshua saw them depart from Shiloh.[1] It was not merely that to himself it would seem like the beginning of the end, but that misgivings and fears could not but crowd upon his mind. They parted from Shiloh to comparatively far distances, to be separated from their brethren by Jordan, and scattered amid the wide tracts, in which their nomadic pastoral life would bring them into frequent and dangerous contact with heathen neighbours. They were now united to their brethren; they had fought by their side; would this union continue? The very riches with which they departed to their distant homes (xxii. 8) might become a source of danger. They had parted with Jehovah's blessing and monition from the central sanctuary at Shiloh. Would it remain such to them, and they preserve the purity of their faith at a distance from the tabernacle and its services? Joshua remembered only too well the past history of Israel; he knew that even now idolatry, although publicly non-existent, had still its roots and fibres in many a household as a sort of traditional superstition (xxiv. 23). Under such circumstances it was that strange tidings reached Israel and Joshua. Just before crossing Jordan the two and a half tribes had built an altar that could be seen far and wide, and then departed without leaving any explanation of their conduct. At first sight this would have seemed in direct contravention of one of the

---

[1] From Josh. xxii. 9 we learn that they "departed out of Shiloh," hence after the land had been finally apportioned among the tribes. Of course, this does not imply that the *same* warriors had continued all through the wars without changing.

first principles of Israel's worship. Place, time, and manner of it were all God-ordained and full of meaning, and any departure therefrom, even in the slightest particular, destroyed the meaning, and with it the value of all. More especially would this appear an infringement of the express commands against another altar and other worship (Lev. xvii. 8, 9; Deut. xii. 5–7), to which the terrible punishment of extermination attached (Deut. xiii. 12–18). And yet there was something so strange in rearing this altar on the *western* side of the Jordan,[1] and not on the eastern, and in their own possession, that their conduct, however blameworthy, might possibly bear another explanation than that of the great crime of apostacy.

It was an anxious time when the whole congregation gathered, by their representatives, at Shiloh, not to worship, but to consider the question of going to war with their own brethren and companions in arms, and on such grounds. Happily, before taking decided action, a deputation was sent to expostulate with the two and a half tribes. It consisted of ten princes, representatives, each of a tribe, and all "heads of houses of their fathers," though, of course, not the actual chiefs of their tribes. At their head was Phinehas, the presumptive successor to the high priesthood, to whose zeal, which had once stayed the plague of Peor, the direction might safely be left. We are not told how they gathered the representatives of the offending tribes, but the language in which, as recorded, the latter were addressed, is quite characteristic of Phinehas.

The conduct of the two and a half tribes had been self-willed and regardless of one of the first duties—that of not giving offence to the brethren, nor allowing their liberty to become a stumbling-block to others. For a doubtful good they had committed an undoubted offence, the more unwarranted,

[1] This we gather from xxii. 10: "And when they came to the circle (circuits) of Jordan, that is in the land of Canaan" (in contrast to "the land of Gilead"), ver. 9. Again in ver. 11: "built an altar in face (or, in front) of the land of Canaan (that is, at its extreme boundary, looking towards it), in the circuits of Jordan, by the side of (or, 'over against') the children of Israel."

that they had neither asked advice nor offered explanation. Phinehas could scarcely help assuming that they had "committed unfaithfulness towards the God of Israel."[1] He now urged upon them the remembrance, yet fresh in their minds, of the consequences of the sin of Peor, and which had, alas! still left its bitter roots among the people.[2] If, on account of their uncleanness, they felt as if they needed nearer proximity to the altar, he invited them back to the western side of the Jordan, where the other tribes would make room for them. But if they persisted in their sin, he reminded them how the sin of the one individual, Achan, had brought wrath on all the congregation. If so, then the rest of Israel must take action, so as to clear themselves from complicity in their "rebellion."

In reply, the accused tribes protested, in language of the most earnest expostulation, that their conduct had been wholly misunderstood.[3] So far from wishing to separate from the tabernacle and worship of Jehovah, this great altar had been reared as a witness to all ages that they formed an integral part of Israel, lest in the future they might be debarred from the service of Jehovah. That, and that alone, had been their meaning, however ill expressed. The explanation thus offered was cause of deep thankfulness to the deputies and to all Israel. Thus, in the good providence of God, this cloud also passed away.

A twofold work had been intrusted to Joshua: to *conquer the land* (Josh. i. 8), and to *divide it by inheritance* among the

---

[1] So literally, and not, as in Authorised Version (xxii. 16): "What trespass is this that ye have committed?" This sin is very significantly viewed here as an "unfaithfulness" towards the God of Israel.

[2] So in Josh. xxii. 17. Such a judgment as the death of 24,000 (Numb. xxv. 9) must have left many painful gaps in Israel. But this was not the saddest consequence. For, evidently, the worship of Baal-Peor had struck root among the people, even although for the present it was outwardly suppressed.

[3] There is a fervency of utterance in their protestation, which appears even in the accumulation of the names of God. The particle rendered "if" is here used as the formula for an oath.

people[1] (i. 6). Both had been done, and in the spirit of strength, of courage, and of believing obedience enjoined at the outset (i. 7). Unlike his great predecessor and master, Moses, he had been allowed to finish his task, and even to rest after its completion.[2] And now he had reached one hundred and ten years, the age at which his ancestor Joseph had died (Gen. l. 26). Like a father who thinks of and seeks to provide for the future of his children after his death;[3] like Moses when he gathered up all his life, his mission, and his teaching in his last discourses; as the Apostle Peter, when he endeavoured that Christians might "be able after his Exodus[4] to have these things always in remembrance," so did Joshua care for the people of his charge. On two successive occasions he gathered all Israel, through their representative "elders,"[5] to address to them last words. They are in spirit and even in tenor singularly like those of Moses, as indeed he had no new truth to communicate.

The first assembly must have taken place either in his own city of Timnath-serah,[6] or else at Shiloh. The address there given had precisely the same object as that afterwards delivered by him, and indeed may be described as preparatory to the latter. Probably the difference between the two lies in this, that the first discourse treated of the future of Israel rather in its political aspect, while the second, as befitted the circum-

---

[1] So also the Book of Joshua is divided into two parts: the first (ch. i.-xii.), descriptive of the *conquest*, the second of the *division* of the land.

[2] Joshua seems to have lived about fifteen years after the final division of the land.

[3] This idea is suggested by Calvin.

[4] The word used by the apostle (2 Pet. i. 15) is "*Exodus*," the same as employed in the conversation on the Mount of Transfiguration (Luke ix. 31), to which St. Peter in his epistle makes pointed reference (2 Pet. i. 16-18).

[5] All Israel were summoned through their *elders*, which is a generic name including the three divisions: "heads" of tribes, clans, and houses of fathers, "judges," and "officers."

[6] Literally "the possession of the sun"—properly *Timnath serach*, also called *Timnath-Cheres* (Judges ii. 9) by a transposition of letters, not uncommon in the Hebrew.

stances, chiefly dwelt on the past mercies of Jehovah, and urged upon the people decision in their spiritual choice. Both discourses are marked by absence of all self-exaltation or reference to his own achievements. It is the language of one who, after long and trying experience, could sum up all he knew and felt in these words: "As for me and my house, we will serve Jehovah."

The first discourse of Joshua consisted of two parts (xxiii. 2–13, and 14–16), each beginning with an allusion to his approaching end, as the motive of his admonitions. Having first reminded Israel of all God's benefits and of His promises, in case of their faithfulness, he beseecheth them: "Take heed very much to your souls to love Jehovah your God" (ver. 11), the danger of an opposite course being described with an accumulation of imagery that shows how deeply Joshua felt the impending danger. Proceeding in the same direction, the second part of Joshua's address dwells upon the absolute certainty with which judgment would follow, as surely as formerly blessing had come.

The second address of Joshua, delivered to the same audience as the first, was even more solemn. For, this time, the assembly took place at Shechem, where, on first entering the land, Israel had made solemn covenant by responding from Mounts Ebal and Gerizim to the blessings and the curses enunciated in the law. And the present gathering also was to end in renewal of that covenant. Moreover, it was in Shechem that Abraham had, on entering Canaan, received the first Divine promise, and here he had built an altar unto Jehovah (Gen. xii. 6, 7). Here also had Jacob settled after his return from Mesopotamia, and purged his household from lingering idolatry, by burying their Teraphim under an oak (Gen. xxxiii. 20; xxxv. 2, 4). It was truly a "sanctuary of Jehovah" (Josh. xxiv. 26), and they who came to it "gathered before God"[1] (ver. 1). In language the most tender and impressive, reminding us of Stephen's last speech before the

---

[1] In the Hebrew with the article "the God," to indicate that it was the only true and living *Elohim*.

Sanhedrim (Acts vii.), Joshua recalled to them the mercies of God (Josh. xxiv. 2–13), specially in those five great events: the calling of Abraham, the deliverance from Egypt, the defeat of the Amorites and of the purpose of Balaam,[1] the miraculous crossing of Jordan and taking of Jericho, and finally, the Divine victory[2] given them over all the nations of Canaan. On these grounds he now earnestly entreated them to make decisive choice of Jehovah as their God.[3] And they replied by solemnly protesting their determination to cleave unto the Lord, in language which not only re-echoed that of the preface to the ten commandments (Ex. xx. 2; Deut. v. 6), but also showed that they fully responded to Joshua's appeals. To bring the matter to a clear issue, Joshua next represented to them that they could not serve Jehovah (xxiv. 19)—that is, in their then state of heart and mind—"in their own strength, without the aid of grace; without real and serious conversion from all idols; and without true repentance and faith."[4] To attempt this were only to bring down judgment instead of the former blessing. And when the people still persevered in their profession, Joshua, having made it a condition that they were to put away the strange gods from among them and "direct" their hearts "unto Jehovah, God of Israel,"[5] made again solemn

---

[1] In xxiv. 9: "Then Balak . . . . arose and warred against Israel;" not with outward weapons, but through Balaam.

[2] The expressive figure is here used: "And I sent the hornet before you," to designate that which carries terror among the inhabitants of a place. Comp. Ex. xxiii. 28; Deut. vii. 20.

[3] The call to "choose this day" whom they would serve (ver. 15), does not place the duty of their allegiance to Jehovah in any doubt, but is rather the strongest and most emphatic mode of enforcing the admonition of ver. 14, especially followed, as it is, by the declaration: "but as for me and my house, we will serve Jehovah."

[4] So in substance J. H. Michaelis in his notes on the passage.

[5] Keil argues that the expression (ver. 23), "put away the strange gods which are among you," means "in your hearts." But this interpretation is critically untenable, while such passages as Amos v. 26 and Acts vii. 43 prove the existence of idolatrous rites among the people, even though they may have been discarded in public.

covenant with them. Its terms were recorded in a document which was placed within the book of the Law,[1] and in memory thereof a great stone was set up under the memorable tree at Shechem which had been the silent witness of so many solemn transactions in the history of Israel.

With this event the history of Joshua closes.[2] Looking back upon it, we gather the lessons of his life and work, and of their bearing upon the future of Israel. Born a slave in Egypt, he must have been about forty years old at the time of the Exodus. Attached to the person of Moses, he led Israel in the first decisive battle against Amalek (Ex. xvii. 9, 13), while Moses, in the prayer of faith, held up to heaven the God-given "rod." It was no doubt on that occasion that his name was changed from *Oshea*, "help," to *Jehoshua*, "Jehovah is help" (Numb. xiii. 16). And this name is the key to his life and work. Alike in bringing the people into Canaan, in his wars, and in the distribution of the land among the tribes—from the miraculous crossing of Jordan and taking of Jericho to his last address—he was the embodiment of his new name: "Jehovah is help!" To this outward calling his character also corresponded. It is marked by singleness of purpose, directness, and decision. There is not indeed about him that elevation of faith, or comprehensiveness of spiritual view which we observed in Moses. Witness Joshua's despondency after the first failure at Ai. Even his plans and conceptions lack breadth and depth. Witness his treaty with the Gibeonites, and the commencing disorganisation among the tribes at Shiloh. His strength always lies in his singleness of purpose. He sets an object before him, and unswervingly follows it. So in his campaigns: he marches rapidly, falls suddenly upon the enemy, and follows up the victory with unflagging energy. But there

---

[1] He took, as we would say, "Minutes" of this transaction, which were placed inside the roll of the law of Moses.

[2] The deaths of Joshua and Eleazar were, of course, chronicled at a later period. According to the Talmud (Baba Bathra, 15 a), the former was written down by Eleazar, and the latter by Phinehas.

he stops—till another object is again set before him, which he similarly pursues. The same singleness, directness, and decision, rather than breadth and elevation, seem also to characterise his personal religion.

There is another remarkable circumstance about Joshua. The conquest and division of the land seem to have been his sole work. He does not appear to have even ruled as a judge over Israel. But so far also as the conquest and division of the land were concerned, his work was not complete, nor, indeed, *intended* to be complete. And this is characteristic of the whole Old Testament dispensation, that no period in its history sees its work completed, but only begun and pointing forward to another yet future,[1] till at last all becomes complete in the "fulness of time" in Christ Jesus. Thus viewed, a fresh light is cast upon the name and history of Joshua. Assuredly Joshua did not give "*rest*" even to his own generation, far less to Israel as a nation. *It was rest begun, but not completed*—a rest which even in its temporal aspect left so much unrest; *and as such it pointed to Christ.* What the one Joshua could only begin, not really achieve, even in its outward typical aspect, pointed to, and called for the other Joshua, the Lord Jesus Christ,[2] in Whom and by Whom all is reality, and all is perfect, and all is rest for ever. And so also it was only after many years that *Oshea* became Joshua, while the name Joshua was given to our Lord by the angel before His birth (Matt. i. 21). The first *became*, the second *was* Joshua. And so the name and the work of Joshua pointed forward to the fulness in Christ, alike by what it was and by what it was not, and this in entire accordance with the whole character and object of the Old Testament.

[1] See some interesting remarks in Herzog's *Real Encycl.*, vol. vii. p. 41. If any reader, able to follow out such questions, should feel interested in "the higher criticism" of the Book of Joshua, we would direct him to the masterly essay by L. König, in *Alttest. Studien*, part i.

[2] Jesus is the Greek equivalent for Joshua.

CHAPTER XIII.

Summary of the Book of Judges—Judah's and Simeon's Campaign—Spiritual and national Decay of Israel—"From Gilgal to Bochim."

(JUDGES I.–III. 4.)

IF evidence were required that each period of Old Testament history points for its completion to one still future, it would be found in the Book of Judges. The history of the three and a half centuries which it records brings not anything new to light, either in the life or history of Israel; it only continues what is already found in the Book of Joshua, carrying it forward to the Books of Samuel, and thence through Kings, till it points in the dim distance to *the King* of Israel, the Lord Jesus Christ, Who gives perfect rest in the perfect kingdom. In the Book of Joshua we see two grand outstanding facts, one explaining the outer, the other the inner history of Israel. As for the latter, we learn that ever since the sin of Peor, if not before, idolatry had its hold upon the people. Not that the service of the Lord was discarded, but that it was combined with the heathen rites of the nations around. But as true religion was really the principle of Israel's national life and unity, "unfaithfulness" towards Jehovah was also closely connected with tribal disintegration, which, as we have seen, threatened even in the time of Joshua. Then, as for the outer history of Israel, we learn that the completion of their possession of Canaan was made dependent on their faithfulness to Jehovah Just as the Christian can only continue to stand by the same faith in which, in his conversion to God, he first had access to Him (Rom. v. 2), so Israel could only retain the land and complete its conquest by the same faith in which they had at first entered it. For faith is never a thing of the past. And for this reason God allowed a remnant of those nations to continue in the land " to prove Israel by them "[1] (Judges iii. 1), so that, as Joshua had forewarned them (Josh. xxiii. 10–16, comp. Judges ii. 3), "faithfulness" on their part would lead to sure and easy victory, while the opposite would end in terrible national disaster. Side by side with these two facts, there is yet a third, and that the most important: the unchanging faithfulness of the Lord, His unfailing pity and lovingkindness, according to which, when Israel was brought low and again turned to Him, He "raised them up judges, ... and delivered them out of the hand of their enemies all the days of the judge" (Judges ii. 18).

The exhibition of these three facts forms the subject-matter of Israel's history under the Judges, as clearly indicated in Judges ii. 21, iii. 4. Accordingly, we must not expect in the Book of Judges a complete or successive history of Israel during these three and half centuries, but rather the exhibition and development of those three grand facts. For Holy Scripture furnishes not —like ordinary biography or history—a chronicle of the lives of individuals, or even of the successive history of a period, save in so far as these are connected with the progress of the kingdom of God. Sacred history is primarily that of the kingdom of God, and only secondarily that of individuals or periods. More particularly is this the reason why we have no record at all of five of the Judges[2]—not even that Jehovah had raised them up. For this cause also some events are specially selected in the sacred narrative, which, to the superficial reader, may seem trivial; sometimes even difficult or objectionable. But a more careful study will show that the real object of these narratives is, to bring into full view one or other of the great principles of

---

[1] This is not in any way inconsistent with Ex. xxiii. 29, etc., Deut. vii. 22. For, as Keil rightly remarks, there is a vast difference between exterminating the whole of the ancient inhabitants of the land, say, in one year, and suspending even their gradual extermination.

[2] *Tola* (x. 1), *Jair* (x. 3), *Ibzan*, *Elon*, and *Abdon* (xii. 8–15).

the Old Testament dispensation. For the same reason also we must not look for strict chronological arrangement in the narratives. In point of fact, the Judges ruled only over one or several of the tribes, to whom they brought special deliverance. Accordingly, the history of some of the Judges overlaps each other, their reign having been contemporaneous in different parts of the land. Thus while in the far east across Jordan the sway of the children of Ammon lasted for eighteen years, till Jephthah brought deliverance (Judges x. 6–xii. 7), the Philistines at the same time oppressed Israel in the far south-west. This circumstance renders the chronology of the Book of Judges more complicated.

The Book of Judges divides itself into three parts: *a general introduction* (i.–iii. 6), *a sketch of the period of the Judges* (iii. 7–xvi. 31), arranged in six groups of events (iii. 7–11; iii. 12–31; iv., v.; vi.–x. 5; x. 6–xii. 15; xiii.–xvi.), *and a double Appendix* (xvii.–xxi.). The two series of events, recorded in the latter, evidently took place at the *commencement* of the period of the Judges. This appears from a comparison of Judges xviii. 1 with i. 34, and again of Judges xx. 28 with Josh. xxii. 13 and xxiv. 33. The first of the two narratives is mainly intended to describe the *religious*, the second the *moral* decadence among the tribes of Israel. In these respects they throw light upon the whole period. We see how soon, after the death of Joshua and of his contemporaries, Israel declined—*spiritually*, in combining with the heathen around, and mingling their idolatrous rites with the service of Jehovah; and *nationally*, the war with the Canaanites being neglected, and the tribes heeding on every great occasion only their private interests and jealousies, irrespective of the common weal (v. 15–17, 23; viii. 1–9), until "the men of Ephraim" actually levy war against Jephthah (xii. 1–6), and Israel sinks so low as to deliver its *Samson* into the hands of the Philistines (xv. 9–13)!

Side by side with this decay of Israel we notice a similar decline in the *spiritual* character of the Judges from an *Othniel* and a *Deborah* down to *Samson*. The mission of these Judges was, as we have seen, chiefly local and always temporary, God raising up a special deliverer in a time of special need. It is quite evident that such special instruments were not necessarily always under the influence of spiritual motives. God has at all periods of history used what instruments He pleased for the deliverance of His people—a Darius, a Cyrus, a Gamaliel, and in more modern times often what appeared the most unlikely, to effect His own purposes. Yet in the history of the Judges it seems always the best and most religious whom the locality or period affords who is chosen, so that the character of the Judges affords also an index of the state of a district or period. And in each of them we mark the presence of real faith (Heb. xi.), acting as the lever-power in their achievements, although their faith is too often mingled with the corruptions of the period. *The Judges were Israel's representative men*—representatives of its faith and its hope, but also of its sin and decay. Whatever they achieved was "by faith." Even in the case of Samson, all his great deeds were achieved in the faith of God's gift to him as a Nazarite, and when "the Spirit of the Lord came upon him." Hence the Judges deserved to be enrolled in the catalogue of Old Testament "worthies." Besides, we must not forget the necessary influence upon them of the spirit of their age. For we mark in the Bible a progressive development, as the light grew brighter and brighter unto the perfect day. In truth, if this were not the case, one of two inferences would follow. Either we would be tempted to regard its narratives as partial, or else be driven to the conclusion that these men could not have been of the period in which they are placed, since they had nothing in common with it, and hence could neither have been leaders of public opinion, nor even been understood by it.

From these brief preliminary observations we turn to notice, that there were altogether twelve, or rather, including Deborah (Judges iv. 4), thirteen Judges over Israel. Of only eight of these are any special deeds recorded. The term Judge must not, however, be regarded as primarily referring to the ordinary judicial functions, which were discharged by the elders and officers of every tribe and city. Rather do we regard it as equivalent to *leader* or *ruler*. The period of the Judges closes with Samson. Eli was mainly high priest, and only in a secondary sense "Judge," while Samuel formed the transition from the Judges to royalty. With Samson the period of the Judges reached at the same time its highest and its lowest point. It is as a *Nazarite*, devoted to God before his birth, that he is "Judge," and achieves his great feats—and it is as a Nazarite that he falls and fails through selfishness and sin. In both respects he is the representative of Israel—God-devoted, a Nazarite people, and as such able to do all things, yet falling and failing through spiritual adultery. And thus the period of the Judges ends as every other period. It contains the germ of, and points to something better; but it is imperfect, incomplete, and fails, though even in its failure it points forward. Judges must be succeeded by kings, and kings by *the* King—the true Nazarite, the Lord Jesus Christ.

The period between the death of Joshua and the first "Judge" is summarised in Judges i.-iii. 6. It appears, that under the influence of Joshua's last address, deepened no doubt by his death, which followed soon afterwards, the "holy war" was resumed. In this instance it was purely aggressive on the part of Israel, whereas formerly, as a matter of fact, the attack always came from the Canaanites (except in the case of Jericho and of Ai). But the measure of the sin of the nations who occupied Palestine was now full (Gen. xv. 13-16), and the storm of judgment was to sweep them away. For this purpose Israel, to whom God in His mercy had given the land, was to be employed—but only in so far as the people realised its calling to dedicate the land unto the Lord. On the ruins of what not only symbolised, but at the time really was the kingdom of Satan,[1] the theocracy was to be upbuilt. Instead

---

[1] It is difficult to resist the impression that Canaan was not only the focus of ancient heathenism in its *worst* abominations, but the centre whence it spread. Very much in the mythology, and almost all the vileness of Greek and Roman heathenism is undoubtedly of Canaanitish origin.

of that focus whence the vilest heathenism overspread the world, the kingdom of God was to be established, with its opposite mission of sending the light of truth to the remotest parts of the earth. Nor can it be difficult to understand how, in such circumstances, at such a time, and at that period of religious life, any compromise was impossible—and every war must be one of extermination.

Before entering on this new "war," the children of Israel asked Jehovah, no doubt through the *Urim* and *Thummim*, which tribe was to take the lead. In reply, Judah was designated, in accordance with ancient prophecy (Gen. xlix. 8). Judah, in turn, invited the co-operation of Simeon, whose territory had been parcelled out of its own. In fact, theirs were common enemies. The two tribes encountered and defeated the Canaanites and Perizzites in *Bezek*, a name probably attaching to a district rather than a place, and, as the word seems to imply, near the shore of the Dead Sea.[1] In the same locality *Adoni-bezek*[2] appears to have made a fresh stand, but with the same disastrous result. On that occasion a remarkable, though most cruel retaliation overtook him. As chieftain of that district he must have been equally renowned for his bravery and cruelty. After a custom not uncommon in antiquity,[3] the many chieftains whom he had subdued were kept, like dogs "for lengthened sport,"[4] under the banqueting table of the proud conqueror in a mutilated condition, their thumbs and great toes cut off, in token that they could never

---

Indeed, we may designate the latter as the only real *missionary* heathenism at the time in the world. Consider the significance of planting in its stead the kingdom of God, with its untold missionary influences and its grand purpose to the world! We must also bear in mind, that the spread of Canaanitish idolatry would be greatly promoted by the chain of colonies which extended from Asia Minor into Europe.

[1] Cassel derives the name from the slimy nature of the soil.

[2] According to Cassel: "My god is splendour," perhaps a sun worshipper.

[3] Cassel enumerates many such.

[4] "*In longum sui ludibrium,*" Curtius de Rebus: Alex. v. 5, 6.

again handle sword and bow, nor march to war. It need scarcely be said, that the Mosaic law never contemplated such horrors. Nevertheless the allied tribes now inflicted mutilation upon Adoni-bezek. The victors carried him to Jerusalem, where he died. On that occasion the city itself, so far as it lay within the territory of Judah, was taken and burnt. But the boundary line between Judah and Benjamin ran through Jerusalem, the Upper City and the strong castle, which were held by the Jebusites, being within the lot of Benjamin. In the war under Joshua, the Jebusites had foiled Judah (Josh. xv. 63). Now also they retired to their stronghold, whence the Benjamites did not even attempt to dislodge them (Judges i. 21). From Jerusalem the tribes continued their victorious march successively to "the mountain," or highlands of Judah, then to the *Negeb*, or south country, and finally to the *Shephelah*, or lowlands, along the sea-shore. Full success attended the expedition, the tribes pursuing their victories as far south as the utmost borders of the ancient kingdom of Arad, where, as their fathers had vowed (Numb. xxi. 2), they executed the ban upon *Zephath* or *Hormah*. The descendants of Hobab (Judges iv. 11) the Kenite,[1] the brother-in-law of Moses, who had followed Israel to Canaan (Numb. x. 29), and had since pitched their tents near Jericho, now settled in this border land, as best suited to their nomadic habits and previous associations (Judges i. 8–11, 16). The campaign ended[2] with the incursion into the *Shephelah*, where Judah wrested from the Philistines three out of their five great cities. This conquest, however, was not permanent (xiv. 19; xvi. 1), nor were the inhabitants of the valley driven out, "because they had chariots of iron."[3]

But the zeal of Israel did not long continue. In fact, all

---

[1] This notice is here inserted, probably, because the event happened between the taking of Debir (i. 11) and that of Zephath (i. 17).

[2] Only Gaza, Ashkelon, and Ekron seem to have been taken, but neither Gath nor Ashdod.

[3] These were armed with scythes on their wheels.

that follows after the campaign of Judah and Simeon is a record of failure and neglect, with the single exception of the taking of Bethel by the house of Joseph. Thus the tribes were everywhere surrounded by a fringe of heathenism. In many parts, Israelites and heathens dwelt together, the varying proportions among them being indicated by such expressions as that the "Canaanites dwelt among" the Israelites, or else the reverse. Sometimes the Canaanites became tributary. On the other hand, the Amorites succeeded in almost wholly [1] driving the tribe of Dan out of their possessions, which induced a considerable proportion of the Danites to seek fresh homes in the far north (Judges xviii.).

Israel was settling down in this state, when their false rest was suddenly broken by the appearance among them of "the Angel of Jehovah."[2] No Divine manifestation had been vouchsafed them since the Captain of Jehovah's host had stood before Joshua in the camp at Gilgal (Josh. v. 13-15). And now, at the commencement of a new period, and that one of spiritual decay, He "came" from Gilgal to Bochim, not to announce the miraculous fall of a Jericho before the ark of Jehovah, but the continuance of the heathen power near them in judgment upon their unfaithfulness and disobedience. "From Gilgal to Bochim!" There is much in what these names suggest—and that even although Gilgal may have been the permanent camp,[3] where leading representatives of the nation were always assembled, to whom "the Angel of Jehovah" in the first place addressed Himself, and *Bochim*, or "weepers," the designation given afterwards to the meeting-place by the ancient sanctuary (either Shechem or more probably Shiloh), where the elders of the people gathered to hear the Divine message. And truly what had passed between the entrance into Canaan and that

---

[1] They drove them out of the valley (i. 35) which constituted the principal part of the possession of Dan (Josh. xix. 40). The Amorites even "dared to dwell" in Har-Heres, in Aijalon, and in Shaalbim (Judges i. 35), although they were afterwards made tributary by the house of Joseph.

[2] Cassel erroneously regards this as a human messenger from God.

[3] For the situation of this Gilgal, comp. a previous chapter.

period might be thus summed up: "From Gilgal to Bochim!" The immediate impression of the words of the Angel of Jehovah was great. Not only did the place become *Bochim*, but a sacrifice was offered unto Jehovah, for wherever His presence was manifested, there might sacrifice be brought (comp. Deut. xii. 5; Judges vi. 20, 26, 28; xiii. 16; 2 Sam. xxiv. 25).

But, alas! the impression was of but short continuance. Mingling with the heathen around, "they forsook Jehovah, and served Baal and Ashtaroth."[1] Such a people could only learn in the school of sorrow. National unfaithfulness was followed by national judgments. Yet even so, Jehovah, in His mercy, ever turned to them when they cried, and raised up "deliverers." In the truest sense these generations "had not known all the wars of Canaan" (Judges iii. 1). For the knowledge of them is thus explained in the Book of Psalms (Ps. xliv. 2, 3): "Thou didst drive out the heathen with Thy hand, and plantedst them; Thou didst afflict the nations, and cast them out. For they got not the land in possession by their own sword, neither did their own arm save them: but Thy right hand, and Thine arm, and the light of Thy countenance, because Thou hadst a favour unto them." This lesson was now to be learned in bitter experience by the presence and power of the heathen around: "to prove Israel by them, to know whether they would hearken unto the commandments of Jehovah, which He commanded their fathers by the hand of Moses" (Judges iii. 4).

[1] *Ashtaroth* is the "star-goddess" of the night, *Astarte*, whose symbol, properly speaking, was the *Asherah*. It is impossible to detail the vileness of her service. Mention of it occurs so early as in Gen. xiv. 5, where we read of *Ashteroth Karnaim*, the "star-goddess of the horns," *i.e.*, the quarter of the moon.

CHAPTER XIV.

Othniel—Ehud—Shamgar.

(JUDGES III. 5-31.)

THE first scene presented in the history of the Judges is that of Israel's intermarriage with the heathen around, and their doing "evil in the sight of Jehovah," forgetting Him, and serving "Baalim and the groves."[1] And the first "judgment" on their apostasy is, that they are "sold" by the Lord into the hand of "Chushan-rishathaim, king of Mesopotamia," or rather of "Aram-naharaim," "the highland by the two streams" (Euphrates and Tigris). Curiously enough, there is an ancient Persian tradition, according to which the monarchs of Iran, who held dominion "by the streams," waged war against Egypt, Syria, and Asia Minor. Of their heroes, who are described as *Cushan*, or from the land of *Chusistan* (= Scythians, Parthians?), the most notable is *Rustan* or *Rastim*, a name evidently akin to Rishathaim.[2] And so ancient heathen records once more throw unexpected light upon the historical narratives of the Old Testament.

The oppression had lasted full eight years when Israel "cried[3] unto Jehovah." The deliverer raised up for them was *Othniel*, the younger brother of Caleb, whose bravery had formerly gained him the hand of his wife (i. 12-15). But his success now was not due to personal prowess. "The Spirit of

---

[1] "Baalim and the Astartes" (Ashtaroth or Asheroth). So literally.
[2] See Cassel's *Comm.* p. 33. Jewish tradition and most commentators translate the name: "twofold sin," in supposed allusion to a twofold wrong against Israel. But this is, to say the least, a very strained explanation.
[3] The same word as that used of Israel in Ex. ii. 23.

Jehovah was[1] upon him, and he judged Israel, and went out to war." For the first time in the Book of Judges we meet here the statement, that "the Spirit of Jehovah" "was upon," or "clothed," or else "came upon" a person. We naturally connect the expression with what we read of "the manifold gifts of the Spirit" as these are detailed in Is. xi. 2, which were distributed to each as God pleased, and according to the necessity of the time (1 Cor. xii. 11). But, in thinking of these influences, we ought to bear two things in mind. *First:* although, in each case, the influence came straight from above—from the Spirit of God—for the accomplishment of a special purpose, it was *not* necessarily, as under the New Testament dispensation, a sanctifying influence. *Secondly:* this influence must not be regarded as the same with the *abiding* presence of the Holy Spirit in the heart. This also belongs to the New Testament dispensation. In short, these gifts of the Holy Spirit were *miraculous*, rather than *gracious*—like the gifts in the early Church, rather than as "the promise of the Father." In the case of Othniel, however, we note that the Spirit of God "*was* upon" him, and that, under His influence, "he judged" Israel, even "before he went out to war." And so, while ancient Jewish tradition in all other instances paraphrases the expression, "the Spirit of the Lord," by "the spirit of strength," in the case of *Othniel*—"the lion of God"[2]—it renders it: "the spirit of prophecy." A war so undertaken must have been successful, and "the land had rest forty years."[3]

---

[1] The expression here and in xi. 29 is, "was upon" him; in vi. 34, it is "clothed him;" in xiv. 6, 19; xv. 14, "came upon" or "lighted upon." The attentive reader will note the important difference of meaning in each of these terms. In the first case there is permanence—at least to carry out a special purpose; in the second, the idea is of surrounding, protecting, or enduing; and, in the third, of suddenness, implying a power, wholly from without, descending unexpectedly at the right moment, and then withdrawn. All have, however, this in common, that the influence comes straight from the Spirit of God.

[2] This, or else "my lion is God," is the rendering of the name.

[3] The text does not make it clear whether Othniel died at the end of these forty years; only that he died after the land had obtained rest.

The next judgment to rebellious Israel came likewise from the east. Quite on the eastern boundary of Reuben and of Gad lay the land of Moab. One of the chieftains of its tribes, Eglon,[1] now allied himself with the old enemies of Israel, Ammon and Amalek, the former occupying the territory south of Reuben, the latter the districts in the far south-west, below Philistia. Eglon swept over the possessions of the trans-Jordanic tribes, crossed the river, and made Jericho, which was probably rebuilt as a town, though not as a fortress, his capital. Having thus cut the land, as it were, into two, and occupied its centre and garden, Eglon reduced Israel for eighteen years to servitude. At the end of that period the people once more "cried unto the Lord," and "the Lord raised them up a deliverer," although Holy Scripture does *not* say that in his mode of deliverance he acted under the influence of the Spirit of the Lord. In the peculiar circumstances of the case this silence is most significant.

The "deliverer" was "Ehud (probably, the praised one), the son of Gera, a Benjamite, a man left-handed," or, as the original has it, "shut up"[2] or "weak" "as to his right hand." The conspiracy against Eglon was well planned. Ehud placed himself at the head of a deputation charged to bring Eglon "a present," or, more probably, the regular tribute, as we gather from the similar use of the word in 2 Sam. viii. 2, 6;

[1] We infer that Eglon was not the king of all Moab, because in that case he would not have exchanged its capital Rabbath Moab for Jericho, and also from the fact that, after the death of Eglon and the destruction of his garrison, the war does not seem to have been carried on by either party.

[2] Not paralysed—the term occurs in Ps. lxix. 15. Cassel has some very curious remarks on this subject. *Benjamin* means "son of the right hand;" yet it seems a peculiarity of Benjamin to have had left-handed warriors (see Judges xx. 16). Similarly we read of certain African races, that they mostly fought with the left hand (Stobæus, *Ecl. phys.* i. 52). The Roman hero, who, like Ehud, delivered his country of its foreign oppressor, was Scævola—left-handed. The left was in ancient times the place of honour, because it was the weaker and less protected side (Xenoph. Cyrop. viii. 4). Similarly, the sea (in Hebrew, *yam*) was always regarded as the *right* side of a country—that of liberty, as it were.

2 Kings xvii. 3, 4. But Ehud carried under his raiment a two-edged dagger, a cubit long; according to the LXX translation, about three-quarters of a foot. The tribute was delivered, no doubt with many protestations of humility and allegiance [1] on the part of Ehud, and the deputation graciously dismissed. It was needful for his plan, and probably in accordance with his wish to involve no one else in the risk, that the rest should be done by Ehud alone. Having seen his fellow-countrymen safely beyond "the quarries that were by Gilgal," or, rather, as the term implies, beyond "the terminal columns" (always objects of idolatrous worship), that divided the territory of Eglon from that of Israel, he returned to the king, whose confidence his former appearance had no doubt secured. The narrative here is exceedingly graphic. The king is no longer in the palace where the deputation had been received, but in his "upper chamber of cooling," [2] a delicious summer-retreat built out upon the end of the flat roof. Ehud professes to have "a secret errand," which had brought him back when his companions were gone. All the more that he does not ask for the withdrawal of the king's attendants does Eglon bid him be "Silent!" in their presence, which, of course, is the signal for their retirement. Alone with the king, Ehud saith, in a manner not uncommon in the East: "I have a message from God unto thee," on which Eglon, in token of reverence, rises from his seat.[3] This is the favourable moment, and, in an instant, Ehud has plunged his dagger up to the hilt into the lower part of his body, with such force that the blade came out behind.[4] Not pausing for a moment, Ehud retires, closes and locks the doors upon the murdered king, and escapes beyond the boundary. Meanwhile the king's attendants, finding the room locked, have waited, till,

[1] The term used here is the same as ordinarily employed for the offering of gifts and sacrifices to the Deity.
[2] So literally.
[3] It was common in antiquity to rise when receiving a direct message from the king. This is the origin of the liturgical practice of rising when the Gospel is read.
[4] The text means only this, and not as in the Authorised Version.

at last, they deem it necessary to break open the doors. The horror and confusion consequent upon the discovery of the murder have given Ehud still further time. And now the preconcerted signal is heard. The shrill blast of the trumpet in *Seirath* (perhaps the "hairy" or "wooded") wakes the echoes of Mount Ephraim. All around from their hiding troop the men of Israel. The first object is to haste back towards Jericho and take the fords of Jordan, so as to allow neither help to come, nor fugitives to escape; the next to destroy the garrison of Moab. In both, Israel are successful, and, " at that time "—of course, not on that precise day—10,000 of Moab are slain, all of them, as we should say, fine men and brave soldiers. " And the land had rest fourscore years."

Ancient history, both Greek and Roman, records similar stories,[1] and, where the murderer has been a patriot, elevates him to the highest pinnacle of heroism. Nay, even Christian history records like instances, as in the murder of Henry III. and Henry IV. of France, the former, even in its details, so like the deed of Ehud. But strikingly different from the toleration, and even commendation, of such deeds by the Papacy[2] is the judgment of the Old Testament. Its silence is here severest condemnation. It needed not cunning and murder to effect deliverance. Not one word of palliation or excuse is said for this deed. It was *not* under the influence of "the Spirit of Jehovah" that such deliverance was wrought, nor is it said of Ehud, as of Othniel, that he "judged Israel." Even Jewish tradition[3] compares Ehud to the "ravening wolf," which had been the early emblem of his tribe, Benjamin (Gen. xlix. 27).

It must have been during this period of eighty years' rest,[4] that another danger at least threatened Benjamin. This time it came from an opposite direction—from the west, where the

---

[1] Thucyd. vi. 56; Polyb. v. 81; Plut. Cæsar, 86; Curtius, vii. 2, 27; comp. Cassel, *u.s.*
[2] Ranke, *Französ. Gesch.* i. p. 171; 473.
[3] Ber. Rabba, c. 89.
[4] This view is also taken by Jewish interpreters, though not by Josephus.

Philistines held possession. "After" Ehud (iii. 31), that is, after his example, a notable exploit was performed by *Shamgar* ("the name of a stranger"?). Under the impulse of sudden sacred enthusiasm, he seized, as the first weapon to hand, an ox-goad, commonly used to urge on the oxen in ploughing. The weapon is formidable enough, being generally about eight feet long, and six inches round at the handle, which is furnished with an iron horn to loosen the earth off the plough, while the other end is armed with a long iron spike. With this weapon he slew no fewer than 600 Philistines, whom, probably, panic seized on his appearance.[1] The exploit seems to have been solitary, and we read neither of further war, nor yet of Shamgar's rule, only that for the time the danger of a Philistine incursion was averted.

CHAPTER XV.

The Oppression of Jabin and Sisera—Deborah and Barak—The Battle of Taanach—The Song of Deborah.

(JUDGES IV., V.)

DARKER and darker are the clouds which gather around Israel, and stranger and more unexpected is the deliverance wrought for them. It had begun with *Othniel*, truly a "lion of God." But after the "lion of God" came one left-handed, then a woman, then the son of an idolater, and then an outlaw of low birth, as if it were ever to descend lower and lower, till the last stage is reached in the Nazarite, Samson, who, as Nazarite, is the typical representative of Israel's calling and strength, and, as Samson, of Israel's weakness and spiritual adultery. Yet each period and each deliverance has its characteristic features and high points.

The narrative opens as if to resume the thread of Israel's

[1] Greek legend has a similar story of Lycurgos chasing Dionysos and the Bacchantes with an ox-goad (*Il.* vi. 135).

continuous history, only temporarily broken by Ehud's life: "And the children of Israel continued[1] to do evil in the eyes of Jehovah—and Ehud was dead." This furnished a long wished-for opportunity. It had been about a century before when a Jabin ("the prudent" or "understanding,"—no doubt the monarch's title, like Pharaoh or Abimelech) had marshalled the chieftains of Northern Palestine against Joshua, and been signally defeated (Josh. xi. 1-10). Since then his capital had been restored and his power grown, till now it seemed the fitting moment to recover his ancient empire. As we understand the narrative, the hosts of Jabin had swept down from *Hazor* in the far north, and occupied the possessions of Naphtali, Zebulun, and Issachar. While Jabin himself continued in his capital, his general, *Sisera* ("mediation," "lieutenant"?) held the southern boundary of the annexed provinces, making his head-quarters at *Harosheth ha Gojim*—"the smithy of the nations"—perhaps so called from being the arsenal where his iron war-chariots, armed with scythes, were made. The site of this place is probably somewhere in the neighbourhood of Bethshean, which afterwards formed the southernmost point of Galilee. Evidently it must have been south of Mount Tabor, to which Barak afterwards marched from Kedron, in the north of Naphtali. For, irrespective of the utterly helpless state of the country, as described in Judges v. 6, Sisera would not have allowed Barak to turn his flank or to march on his rear.[2] The occupation of the north of Palestine by Sisera had lasted twenty years. Relief must have seemed well-nigh hopeless. On the one hand, the population was wholly disarmed (Judges v. 8); on the other, Sisera had no less than nine hundred war-chariots —means of attack which Israel most dreaded. But as often before, so now, suffering led Israel to cry unto the Lord—and help was soon at hand.

[1] So literally, and very significantly for the history of Israel.
[2] For this reason I cannot adopt the localisation proposed by Dr. Thomson (*Land and Book*, ch. xxix.), north of the hills that bound the Plain of Jezreel, although the suggestion is supported by Mr. Grove.

One of the most painful circumstances in the history of the Judges is the utter silence which all this time seems to envelop Shiloh and its sanctuary. No help comes from the priesthood till quite the close of this period. Far away in Mount Ephraim God raised up a woman, on whom He had poured the spirit of prophecy. It is the first time in this history that we read of the prophetic gift. The sacred text conveys, that she exercised it in strict accordance with the Divine law, for it is significantly added in connection with it, that "she judged Israel at that time." *Deborah*, "the bee,"[1] is described as a "burning woman."[2] The meeting-place for all in Israel who sought judgment at her hands was between Ramah and Bethel, under a palm-tree,[3] which afterwards bore her name. Thence she sent for Barak ("lightning,") the son of Abinoam ("my father"—God—"is favour"), from the far north, from Kadesh in Naphtali. His ready obedience proved his preparedness. But when Deborah laid on him the Divine command "gradually to draw"[4] an army of 10,000 men to Mount Tabor, Barak shrank from it, unless Deborah would accompany him. This evidently proved distrust in the result of the undertaking, which in turn showed that he looked for success to the presence of man, rather than entirely to the power of God. Accordingly, he must learn the folly of attaching value to man; and Deborah predicted, that not Israel's leader, but a woman, wholly unconnected with the battle, would have the real triumph.

[1] Although there may be differences as to the mode of its derivation, there is none as to the real import of the name.

[2] The Authorised Version translates "the wife of Lapidoth." The latter word means "torches," and the meaning, as brought out by Cassel, seems to be "a woman of a torch-like spirit;" the Hebrew for wife and woman being the same. Jewish tradition has it, that she was the wife of *Barak*, "lightning," Barak and Lapidoth being, of course, closely connected terms.

[3] The palm-tree was the symbol of Canaan; and the name *Phœnician* is derived from its Greek equivalent.

[4] This is the meaning of the word, as appears from Ex. xii. 21.

Accompanied by Deborah, Barak now returned to Kadesh, whither he summoned the chiefs[1] of Naphtali and Zebulon. All plans being concerted, the combatants converged in small companies, from all roads and directions, "on foot,"[2] towards the trysting-place. About six or eight miles east of Nazareth rises abruptly a beautifully-shaped conical mountain, about 1000 feet high. This is Mount Tabor ("the height"), its sloping sides covered with trees, and affording from its summit one of the most extensive and beautiful prospects in Palestine. Here the army under Barak and Deborah gathered. Tidings soon reached the head-quarters of Sisera. His chariots could of course only fight to advantage in the valleys, and he naturally marched north-west to the plain of Jezreel or Esdraelon. This has ever been, and will prove in the final contest (Rev. xvi. 16), the great battle-field of Israel. It was now the first of many times that its fertile soil was to be watered with the blood of men.

Sisera had chosen his position with consummate skill. Marching in almost straight line upon the plain of Megiddo, his army was now posted at its entrance, resting upon the ancient Canaanitish town of Taanach (Judges v. 19, comp. Josh. xii. 21). Behind, and at his left flank, were the mountains of Manasseh, before him opened the basin of the valley, merging into the plain of Esdraelon, watered by the Kishon. Into this plain must Barak's army descend "on foot," badly armed, without experienced officers, without cavalry or chariots—and here his own 900 war-chariots would operate to best advantage. It was not even like one of those battles in which mountaineers hold their own fastnesses, or swoop down on their enemies in narrow defiles. On the contrary, all seemed to tell against Israel—all but this, that God had previously promised to draw

---

[1] This we infer, as it could not have served any purpose to have gathered the tribes themselves so far north, while it would certainly have attracted the attention of the enemy.

[2] So, and not as the Authorised Version renders it: "he went up with 10,000 men at his feet."

Sisera and his army to the river Kishon, and to deliver them into Barak's hand. Then once more did the Lord appear as "a man of war," and fight on the side of His people. It is said: "And Jehovah discomfited," or rather, "threw into confusion, Sisera and all his chariots, and all his host." The expression is the same as when Jehovah fought against Egypt (Ex. xiv. 25), and again when before Gibeon Joshua bade sun and moon stand still (Josh. x. 10). It indicates the direct interference of the Lord through terrible natural phenomena; (comp. also its use in 2 Sam. xxii. 15; Ps. xviii. 14; cxliv. 6). As we gather from Judges v. 20-22, a fearful storm swept down from heaven in face of the advancing army.[1] The battle must have drawn towards Endor, where its fate was finally decided (Ps. lxxxiii. 9, 10). Presently the war-chariots were thrown into confusion, and instead of being a help became a source of danger. The affrighted horses carried destruction into the ranks of the host. Soon all were involved in a common panic. A scene of wild confusion ensued. It was impossible to retreat, and only in one direction could flight be attempted. And now the waters of Kishon had swollen into a wild torrent which swept away the fugitives![2]

To escape capture, Sisera leaped from his chariot, and fled on foot northwards towards Hazor. Already he had passed beyond Kadesh, and almost reached safety. There the boundary of Naphtali was marked by what was known as "the oakwood at the twin tents of wandering" (Elon be-Zaanannim[3]). Here Heber the Kenite had pitched his tent, having separated from his brethren, who had settled in the extreme south at Arad (Judges i. 16). Living quite on the boundary of Jabin's dominion, and not being really Israelites, the clan of Heber had been left unmolested, and "there was peace between Jabin, king of Hazor, and the house of Heber the Kenite."

---

[1] So also Josephus (*Ant.* v. 5, 6).
[2] The battle must be read in connection with the song of Deborah (Judges v.), which furnishes its details.
[3] Comp. Josh. xix. 33.

Only outward, not real peace! There is something wild and weird about the appearance of these Kenites on the stage of Jewish history. Originally an Arab tribe,[1] they retain to the last the fierceness of their race. Though among Israel, they never seem to amalgamate with Israel, and yet they are more keenly Israelitish than any of the chosen race. In short, these stranger-converts are the most intense in their allegiance to the nation which they have joined, while at the same time they never lose the characteristics of their own race. We mark all this, for example, in the appearance of Jehonadab, the son of Rechab (2 Kings x. 15), and again much later during the troubles that befell Judah in the time of Jeremiah (Jer. xxxv.). Jael, "the chamois," the wife of Heber, was among the Kenites what Deborah, the "torch-woman," was in Israel, only with all the characteristics of her race developed to the utmost. At her tent-door she meets the fugitive Sisera. She disarms his suspicions; she invites him to rest and security; she even sacrifices the sacred rights of hospitality to her dark purpose. There is something terrible and yet grand about that fierce woman, to whom every other consideration is as nothing, so that she may avenge Israel and destroy its great enemy. All seems lawful to her in such an undertaking; every means sanctified by the end in view. She has laid the worn warrior to rest; she has given him for refreshment of the best her tent affords. And now, as he lies in heavy sleep, she stealthily withdraws one of the long iron spikes to which the tent-cords are fastened, and with a heavy hammer once, again, and yet a third time, strikes it into his temples. It is not long before Barak—a "lightning" in pursuit as in battle—has reached the spot. Jael lifts aside the tent-curtain and shows him the gory corpse. In silence Barak turns from the terrible spectacle. But the power of Jabin and his dominion are henceforth for ever destroyed.

There is, as it seems to us, not a word in Scripture to express

---

[1] They were Midianites, descendants of Abraham by Keturah—undoubtedly a Bedouin tribe.

its approbation of so horrible a deed of deceit and violence—no, not even in the praise which Deborah in her song bestows upon Jael. It was not like Deborah's war, nor like Barak's battle, but strictly Kenite. Her allegiance to the cause of the people of God, her courage, her zeal, were Israelitish; their fanatical, wild, unscrupulous manifestation belonged to the race from which she had sprung, to the traditions amidst which she had been nurtured, and to the fiery blood which coursed in her veins—they were not of God nor of His word, but of her time and race. Heathen history tells of similar deeds, and records them with highest praise;[1] Scripture with solemn silence. Yet even so Jehovah reigneth, and the fierce Arab was the sword in His hand!

1. "Then sang Deborah and Barak on that day, saying:

2. For the loose flowing of the long hair,[2]
   For the free dedication of the people,
   Praise ye Jehovah!

3. Hear O kings, hearken O rulers,[3]
   I—to Jehovah will I sing,
   Will psalmody[4] to Jehovah, the God of Israel!

4. Jehovah, when Thou didst come forth from Seir,
   When Thou marchedst from out the fields of Edom,
   The earth trembled, also the heavens dropped,
   Even the clouds dropped water.[5]

---

[1] For example in the case of Aretaphila in Cyrene (Plutarch, *The Virtues of Women*, 19).

[2] The language is extremely difficult, and the most different interpretations have been proposed. We have adopted the ingenious view of Cassel, which represents Israel, as it were, taking the Nazarite vow for God and against His enemies.

[3] Comp. Ps. ii. 2—these, of course, are kings and princes of the heathen.

[4] Always used of sacred song with instrumental accompaniment.

[5] Deborah begins with the record of God's great doings of old in the wilderness, the later parallel being in Ps. lxviii. 7, 8. Comp. here especially Ex. xix. and Deut. xxxiii. 2, and for the expressions, Ps. xlvii. 5; cxiv. 7; Isa. lxiii. 12; lxiv. 2; Jer. x. 10; Joel iii. 16.

5 The mountains quaked before Jehovah—
This Sinai before Jehovah, the God of Israel.[1]

6 In the days of Shamgar, the son of Anath,
In the days of Jael,[2] the highways ceased,[3]
And they who went on paths, went by roundabout ways.

7. Deserted was the open country[4] in Israel—deserted—
Till I arose, Deborah,
I arose a mother in Israel!

8. Chose they new gods—
Then war at the gates—
If shield was seen or spear
Among forty thousand in Israel![5]

9. My heart towards the rulers of Israel,
Those who freely vowed (dedicated) themselves among the people.
Praise ye Jehovah!

10. Ye that ride on white[6] she-asses,
Ye that sit on coverings,[7]
Ye that walk by the way—consider![8]

11. From the noise (sound, voice) of the archers between the draw-wells[9]—

---

[1] Here the *first* stanza of the *first* division of this song ends. There are in all three sections, each of three stanzas. The reader will have no difficulty in marking the progress of thought.

[2] Cassel, as I think fancifully, regards "Jael," not as referring to the wife of Heber, but as a poetic name for Shamgar or Ehud.

[3] Or were deserted.

[4] That is, the country with open villages and towns, in opposition to walled cities.

[5] That is, "shield and spear were *not* seen." So low had the fortunes of Israel fallen before their enemies.

[6] The expression is not without difficulty; Cassel would render it by pack-saddled.

[7] The reference here is evidently to abiding in tents, whether the word be rendered mats, carpets, garments, or coverings.

[8] Viz., the contrast between the insecurity of former times and the present happy condition. Cassel happily points out that, as in Ps. i. 1, the reference is to the three classes: those who sit, who stand, and who go.

[9] The language is very difficult. To us it seems to indicate the contrast between the noise of battle and the peaceful scene of the maidens, who can now go without fear outside the gates to draw water.

There they rehearse the righteous deeds[1] of Jehovah,
The mighty deeds of His open country[2] in Israel—
Then went down to the city gates the people of Jehovah!

Part II.

12. Awake, awake, Deborah,
    Awake, awake—utter the song;
    Arise, Barak, and lead captive thy captives, son of Abinoam!

13. Then went down a remnant of the mighty, of the people,
    Jehovah went down for me among the heroes!

14. From out of Ephraim—his root in Amalek;[3]
    After thee: Benjamin among thy nations[4]—
    From Machir[5] come down they who bear rule,
    From Zebulon who draw out with the staff of the writer.[6]

15. But the princes of Issachar *were* with Deborah—
    And Issachar the foundation[7] of Barak,
    Pouring on foot into the valley!
    By the brooks of Reuben great resolves of heart—[8]

16. Why abodest thou among the folds
    To hear the flutes of the flocks?
    By the brooks of Reuben great ponderings of heart!

17. Gilead dwells on the other side Jordan![9]
    And Dan, why pass upon ships?

---

[1] The righteous deeds are here the *mighty* deeds, and so we have rendered it in the next line.

[2] Seems to mean: His mighty deeds in reference to, or as seen in the villages and unwalled towns of Israel.

[3] There seems an allusion here to the *ancient* glory of the tribes: Ephraim, from which sprang Joshua, the conqueror of Amalek.

[4] "Nations," here equivalent to heathens, and the reference is to Ehud.

[5] Machir is Manasseh, Gen. l. 23.

[6] These two tribes then distinguished for peaceful avocations. Such was the *former* glory of Israel. In the next stanza Deborah proceeds to sketch the *present* state of the tribes.

[7] In his territory the battle was fought—the rendering "foundation" is after the Jewish commentaries.

[8] Here begins the censure of the tribes who should have taken part.

[9] Such is its plea.

Asher sitteth by the sea-shore,
And by its bays resteth!

18. Zebulon a people that jeoparded its life unto death,
And Naphtali on the heights of the field!

---

19. Came kings—warred—
Then warred the kings of Canaan,
In Taanach, by the waters of Megiddo—
Spoil of silver took they none!

20. From heaven warred,
The stars out of their paths warred against Sisera!

21. The river Kishon swept them away,
River of encounters,[1] river Kishon!
March forth my soul in strength!

22. Then clattered the hoofs of the horse
From the racing and chasing[2] of his mighty.

23. Curse ye Meroz,[3] saith the Angel of Jehovah,
Curse ye—cursed its inhabitants,
For they came not to the help of Jehovah,
The help of Jehovah against the mighty!

PART III.

24. Blessed among women, Jael,
The wife of Heber, the Kenite,
Among women in the tent[4] blessed!

25. Water asked he—milk she gave,
In the cup of the noble[5] brought she thickened milk[6]—

---

[1] The common rendering is "ancient river;" Cassel translates "river of help." I prefer "battle," the root being: to meet or to encounter, *obviam ire*. *Kishon*, "the winding one." Ancient Jewish tradition has it that this battle was fought on the Passover, which is not unlikely, as the Kishon is swollen during the rainy season, but quite dry in summer.

[2] In their flight. In the original the word is simply repeated.

[3] Probably a place near Endor, whose inhabitants joined not in the pursuit of Sisera.

[4] Such women as live in tents—pastoral and nomadic, as all the Kenites were.

[5] The cup used on state occasions, as it were.

[6] Cream, or thickened milk (it is a mistake of interpreters to suppose that it was thickened to make him intoxicated); or else camel's milk.

26. Her hand to the tent-nail sendeth forth,
    And her right hand to the ponderous hammer of workmen —
    Hammers[1] she Sisera, shivers[1] his head,
    Cleaves[1] and pierces his temple!

27. Between her feet he winds—he falls—he lies—
    Between her feet he winds—he falls—
    Where he winds there he falls desolated![2]

---

28. High up through the window spies—anxiously she calls,
    The mother of Sisera—cut through the lattice:
    'Why tarrieth his chariot to come,
    Why linger the steps of his war-chariots?'

29. The wise of her princesses answer—
    Nay, she herself answers her words to herself:

30. 'Are they not finding—dividing spoil—
    A maiden—twain maidens to the head of the warriors—
    Spoil of dyed garments to Sisera,
    Spoil of dyed garments—many-coloured kerchief—
    A dyed garment, twain many-coloured kerchiefs for the necks
    of the prey!'[3]

---

31. So perish all Thine enemies, Jehovah—
    And let those who love Him be like the going forth of the sun
    in his strength!

And the land had rest forty years."

---

[1] We almost seem to hear the three strokes of the hammer by which her bloody work is done.

[2] The description of the effects corresponding to the three strokes of the hammer.

[3] With each captive maiden the warrior would also receive one dyed garment and twain many-coloured kerchiefs. In the arduous task of translating this, one of the most difficult passages of Scripture, Cassel's *Commentary* has been of greatest use, although its suggestions are too often fanciful.

CHAPTER XVI.

Midianitish Oppression—The Calling of Gideon—Judgment begins at the House of God—The Holy War—The Night-battle of Moreh.

(JUDGES VI.-VII. 22.)

WITH the calling of Gideon commences the *second* period in the history of the Judges. It lasted altogether less than a century. During its course events were rapidly hastening towards the final crisis. Each narrative is given with full details, so as to exhibit the peculiarity of God's dealings in every instance, the growing apostacy of Israel, and the inherent unfitness even of its best representatives to work real deliverance.

The narrative opens, as those before, with a record of the renewed idolatry of Israel. Judgment came in this instance through the Midianites, with whom the Amalekites and other "children of the east" seem to have combined. It was two hundred years since Israel had avenged itself on Midian (Numb. xxxi. 3-11). And now once more, from the far east, these wild nomads swept, like the modern Bedawîn, across Jordan, settled in the plain of Jezreel, and swooped down as far as Gaza in the distant south-west. Theirs was not a permanent occupation of the land, but a continued desolation. No sooner did the golden harvest stand in the field, or was stored into garners, than they unexpectedly arrived. Like the plague of locusts, they left nothing behind. What they could not carry away as spoil, they destroyed. Such was the feeling of insecurity to life and property, that the people made them " mountain-dens, and caves, and strongholds," where to seek safety for themselves and their possessions. Seven years had this terrible scourge impoverished the land, when the people once more bethought themselves of Jehovah, the God of their fathers, and cried unto Him. This time, however, before granting deliverance, the Lord sent a prophet to bring Israel to a knowledge of their guilt as the source of their misery. The call to repentance was speedily followed by help.

1. *The calling of Gideon.*—Far away on the south-western border of Manasseh, close by the boundary of Ephraim, was the little township of *Ophrah*,[1] belonging to the family of *Abiezer*[2] (Josh. xvii. 2; 1 Chron. vii. 18), apparently one of the smallest clans in Manasseh (Judges vi. 15). Its head or chief was *Joash*—"Jehovah strength," or "firmness." As such he was lord of Ophrah. In such names the ancient spiritual faith of Israel seems still to linger amidst the decay around. And now, under the great oak by Ophrah, suddenly appeared a heavenly stranger. It was the Angel of Jehovah, the Angel of the Covenant, Who in similar garb had visited Abraham at Mamre (Gen. xviii.). Only there He had come, in view of the judgment about to burst, to confirm Abraham's faith—to enter into fellowship with him, while here the object was to call forth faith, and to prove that the Lord was ready to receive the vows and prayers of His people, if they but turned to Him in the appointed way. This may also explain, why in the one case the heavenly visitor joined in the meal,[3] while in the other fire from heaven consumed the offering (comp. Judges xiii. 16; 1 Kings xviii. 38; 2 Chron. vii. 1).

Close by the oak was the winepress of Joash, and there his son *Gideon*[4] was beating out the wheat with a stick.[5] Alike the place and the manner of threshing were quite unusual, and

---

[1] *Ophrah* means township. This Ophrah is to be distinguished from that in Benjamin.   [2] "My father *is* help."

[3] The *Targum* puts it: "they seemed to eat," and Cassel argues that, as theirs was not real humanity, neither was their eating. This, of course, is quite different from the eating on the part of our Lord, which was real— since His humanity and His body were real and true.

[4] "One who cuts down," a warrior.

[5] The term in the original conveys this.

only accounted for by the felt need for secrecy, and the constant apprehension that at an unexpected moment some wild band of Midianites might swoop down upon him. If, as we gather from the Angel's salutation, Gideon was a strong hero, and if, as we infer from his reply, remembrances and thoughts of the former deeds of Jehovah for Israel had burned deep into his heart, we can understand how the humiliating circumstances under which he was working in his father's God-given possession, in one of the remotest corners of the land, must have filled his soul with sadness and longing. It is when "the strong warrior" is at the lowest, that the Messenger of the Covenant suddenly appears before him. Not only the brightness of His face and form, but the tone in which He spake, and still more His words, at once struck the deepest chords in Gideon's heart. "Jehovah with thee, mighty hero!" Then the speaker was one of the few who looked unto Jehovah as the help-giver; and he expressed alike belief and trust! And was there not in that appellation "mighty warrior" a sound like the echo of national expectations—like a call to arms? One thing at least the Angel immediately gained. It was—what the Angel of His Presence *always* first gains—*the confidence of Gideon's heart*. To the unknown stranger he pours forth his inmost doubts, sorrows, and fears. It is not that he is ignorant of Jehovah's past dealings, nor that he questions His present power, but that he believes that, if Jehovah had not withdrawn from Israel, their present calamities could not have rested upon them. The conclusion was right and true, so far as it went; for Israel's prosperity or sufferings depended on the presence or the absence of Jehovah. Thus Gideon's was in truth *a confession of Israel's sin*, and *of Jehovah's justice*. It was *the beginning of repentance*. But Gideon had yet to learn another truth—that Jehovah would turn from His anger, if Israel only turned to Him; and yet another lesson *for himself:* to *put personal trust in the promise of God*, based as it was on His covenant of love, and that whether the outward means to be employed seemed adequate or not.

But Gideon was prepared to learn all this; and, as always, *gradually* did the Lord teach His servant, both by word, and by the sight with which He confirmed it. The reply of the Angel could leave no doubt on the mind of Gideon that a heavenly messenger was before him, Who promised that through him Israel should be saved, and that simply because *He* sent him. It is not necessary to suppose that Gideon understood that this messenger from heaven was the Angel of the Covenant. On the contrary, the revelation was very gradual. Nor do the questions of Gideon seem strange—for such they are rather than doubts. Looking around at his tribe, at his clan, and at his own position in it, help through him seemed most unlikely, and, if we realise all the circumstances, was so. Only one conclusive answer could be returned to all this: "I shall be with thee." The sole doubt now left was: Who was this great I AM?—and this Gideon proposed to solve by "asking for a sign," yet not a sign to his unbelief, but one connected with worship and with sacrifice. Jehovah granted it. As when Moses sought to know God, He revealed not His being but His character and His ways (Ex. xxxiii. 18; xxxiv. 6), so now He revealed to Gideon not only Who had spoken to him, but also that His "Name" was "Jehovah, Jehovah God, merciful and gracious, longsuffering, and abundant in goodness and truth, keeping mercy for thousands, forgiving iniquity, and transgression, and sin."

It would be almost fatal to the proper spiritual understanding of this, as of other Biblical narratives, if we were to transport into it our present knowledge, ideas, and views. Remembering the circumstances of the nation, of Gideon, and of Israel; remembering also the stage of spiritual knowledge attainable at that period, and the difficulty of feeling really sure *Who* the speaker was, we can understand Gideon's request (vi. 1-17): "Work for me a sign that THOU (art He) Who art speaking with me."[1] It is difficult to imagine what special sign Gideon was expecting. Probably he had formed no

[1] So literally.

definite idea. Suffice it, he would bring a sacrificial gift; the rest he would leave to Him. And he brought of the best. It was a kid of the goats, while for the "cakes," to be offered with it, he took a whole ephah of flour, that is, far more than was ordinarily used. But he does all the ministry himself; for no one must know of it. To dispense with assistance, he puts the meat and the cakes in the "bread-basket,"[1] "and the broth in a pot." Directed by the Angel, he spreads his offering on a rock. Then the Angel touches it with the end of His staff; fire leaps out of the rock and consumes the sacrifices; and the Angel has vanished out of his sight. There was in this both a complete answer to all Gideon's questions, and also deep symbolic teaching. But a fresh fear now fills Gideon's heart. Can one like him, who has seen God, live? To this also Jehovah gives an answer, and that for all times: "Peace to thee—fear not—thou shalt not die!" And in perpetual remembrance thereof—not for future worship—Gideon built an altar there,[2] and attached to it the name, "Jehovah-Peace!"

2. One part was finished, but another had to begin. Jehovah had called—would Gideon be ready to obey? For *judgment must now begin at the house of God*. No one is fit for His work in the world till he has begun it in himself and in his own house, and put away all sin and rebellion, however hard the task. It was night when the command of Jehovah came. This time there was neither hesitation nor secrecy about Gideon's procedure. He obeyed God's directions literally and immediately. Taking ten of his servants, he first threw down the altar of Baal, and cut down the *Asherah*—the vile symbol of the vile service of Astarte—that was upon it.[3] One altar was destroyed, but another had to be raised. For, the altar of Jehovah

---

[1] This is the uniform meaning of the word.

[2] The added notice as to its continuance at the time of the writer throws light upon the date of the authorship of the book.

[3] The two were very generally connected, and formed the grossest contrast to the pure service of Jehovah.

could not be reared till that of Baal had been cast down. It was now built, and that not in some secret hiding-place, but on "the top of this defence"—either on the top of the hill on which the fort stood, or perhaps above the place where the people were wont to seek shelter from the Midianites. Upon this altar Gideon offered his father's "second bullock of seven years old"—the age being symbolical of the time of Midian's oppression—at the same time using the wood of the *Asherah* in the burnt-sacrifice. Such a reformation could not, and was not intended to be hidden. The Baal's altar and its Asherah were indeed Joash's, but only as chief of the clan. And when on the following morning the Abiezrites clamoured for the death of the supposed blasphemer, Joash, whose courage and faith seem to have been re-awakened by the bold deed of his son, convinced his clan of the folly of their idolatry by an unanswerable argument, drawn from their own conduct. "What!" he exclaimed, in seeming condemnation, "will ye strive for Baal? Or will ye save him? He that will strive for him let him die until the morrow!"[1] If he be a god, let him strive for himself, because he has thrown down his altar. And they called him on that day Jerubbaal[2] ('let Baal strive'), that is to say, Let the Baal strive with him, because he has thrown down his altar."

3. *The Holy War.*—Gideon had now purified himself and his house, and become ready for the work of the Lord. And yet another important result had been secured. The test to which Baal had been put had proved his impotence. Idolatry had received a heavy blow throughout the land. In Ophrah at least the worship of Jehovah was now alone professed.

---

[1] That is, if any should seek to vindicate Baal to-day let him die; wait till to-morrow to give him time!

[2] In 2 Sam. xi. 21 he is called Jerubbesheth—*besheth*, "shame," being an opprobrious name instead of Baal. May this throw any light on the names of Ishbosheth and Mephibosheth? In 1 Chron. viii. 33, ix. 39, at least Ishbosheth is called Ish-baal, while in 1 Chron. viii. 34 we have Meribbaal ("strife of," or else "against Baal") instead of Mephibosheth ("glory" or "utterance" of Baal).

Moreover, the whole clan Abiezer, and, beyond it, all who had heard of Gideon's deed, perpetuated even in his name, were prepared to look to him as their leader. The occasion for it soon came. Once more the Midianitish Bedawîn had swarmed across Jordan; once more their tents covered the plain of Jezreel. Now or never—now, before their destructive raids once more began, or else never under Gideon—must Israel arise! Yet not of his own purpose did he move. In the deeply expressive language of Scripture: "The Spirit of Jehovah clothed Gideon,"[1] like a garment round about, or rather like an armour. Only after that he blew the trumpet of alarm. First, his own clan Abiezer "was called after him." Next, swift messengers bore the tidings all through Manasseh, and that tribe gathered. Other messengers hastened along the coast (to avoid the Midianites) through Asher northwards to Zebulun and Naphtali, and they as well as Asher, which formerly had not fought with Barak, obeyed the summons.

All was ready—yet one thing more did Gideon seek. It was not from unbelief, nor yet in weakness of faith, that Gideon asked a sign from the Lord, or rather a token, a pledge of His presence. Those hours in the history of God's heroes, when, on the eve of a grand deed of the sublimest faith, the spirit wrestles with the flesh, are holy seasons, to which the superficial criticism of a glib profession, that has never borne the strain of utmost trial, cannot be applied without gross presumption. When in such hours the soul in its agony is seen to cast its burden upon the Lord, we feel that we stand on holy ground. It is like a stately ship in a terrific gale, every beam and timber strained to the utmost, but righting itself at last, and safely reaching port.[2] Or rather it is like a close following of Jesus into the Garden of Gethsemane— with its agony, its prayer, and its victory. In substance, though not in its circumstances, it was the same struggle as

[1] So, Judges vi. 34, literally.
[2] The thought is beautifully carried out in one of the Hymns of St. Joseph of the Studium (translated by Dr. Neale in his *Hymns of the Eastern Church*).

that which was waged in the night when Jacob prayed: "I will not let Thee go except Thou bless me;" the same as when, many centuries afterwards, the Baptist sent his disciples to ask Jesus: "Art Thou He, or do we wait for another?"

The "sign" was of Gideon's own choosing, but graciously accorded him by God. It was twofold. On the first night the fleece of wool spread on the ground was to be full of dew, but the ground all around dry. This, however, might still admit of doubt, since a fleece would naturally attract the dew. Accordingly, the next night the sign was reversed, and the fleece alone remained dry, while the ground all around was wet with dew. The symbolical meaning of the sign is plain. Israel was like that fleece of wool, spread on the wide extent of the nations. But, whereas all the ground around was dry, Israel was filled with the dew, as symbol of the Divine blessing.[1] And the second sign meant, that it was equally of God, when, during Israel's apostasy, the ground all around was wet, and the fleece of Jehovah's flock alone left dry.

4. *The battle:* "*For Jehovah and for Gideon!*"—The faith which had made such trial of God was to be put to the severest trial. Israel's camp was pitched on the height; probably on a crest of Mount Gilboa, which seems to have borne the name of Gilead. At its foot rose "the spring Harod"— probably the same which now bears the name *Jalood*. Beyond it was the hill *Moreh* (from the verb "to indicate," "to direct"), and north of it, in the valley,[2] lay the camp of Midian, 135,000 strong (Judges viii. 10), whereas the number of Israel amounted to only 22,000. But even so they were too many—at least for Jehovah "to give the Midianites into their hand, lest Israel vaunt themselves against Me, saying, Mine own hand hath saved me." In accordance with a previous Divine direction (Deut. xx. 8), proclamation was made for all who were

---

[1] Gen. xxvii. 28; Deut. xxxiii. 13; Prov. xix. 12; Isa. xxvi. 19; Hos. xiv. 5; Mic. v. 7.

[2] "And they camped upon the spring Harod, and the camp of Midian was to him from the north, from the height of Moreh, in the valley" (Judges vii. 1).

afraid, to "turn and wind about[1] from Mount Gilead."[2] Still, Gideon must have been surprised, when, in consequence, he found himself left with only 10,000 men. But even these were too many. To "purify them" (as by refining—for such is the meaning of the word), Gideon was now to bring them down to the spring Harod, where those who were to go to battle would be separated from the rest.[3] All who lapped the water with the tongue out of their hands (out of the hollow hand), as a dog lappeth water, were to go with Gideon, the rest to return, each to his own place. Only three hundred were now left, and with these God declared He would save, and deliver the Midianites into Gideon's hand. If we ask about the rationale of this means of distinction, we conclude, of course, that it indicated the bravest and most ardent warriors,[4] who would not stoop to kneel, but hastily quenched their thirst out of the hollow of their hands, in order to hasten to battle. But Jewish tradition assigns another and deeper meaning to it. It declares that the practice of kneeling was characteristic of the service of Baal, and hence that kneeling down to drink when exhausted betrayed the habit of idolaters. Thus the three hundred would represent those in the host of Israel—"all the knees which have not bowed unto Baal" (1 Kings xix. 18).[5] They who had been selected now "took victuals from the people[6] in their hands, and the trumpets"—the rest were sent away.

[1] So literally; possibly referring to circuitous routes.

[2] Gilead was probably another name for Gilboa. Cassel suggests that it may stand for *Manasseh*.

[3] First the Divine promise, and *then* the Divine command to our faith (Judges vii. 7). So it is always.

[4] Josephus (*Ant.* v. 6, 3) holds, that the three hundred were the most fainthearted. But it is surely unreasonable to suppose that, when all who feared had been dismissed, the most fainthearted should in the end have been chosen.

[5] Cassel attempts to find a special meaning in the comparison: "as a dog licketh," as referring to a kind of dog (of which the ancients and the Talmud speak), which was wont, when the crocodile was asleep, to throw itself into its gullet and to kill it.

[6] This seems to be the real meaning of Judges vii. 8, whether or not it be deemed needful to emendate the text.

That night the small company of Israel occupied an advanced position on the brow of the steep mountain, that overhangs the valley of Jezreel.[1] Effectually concealed, probably by the shelter of wood or vineyards, the vast straggling camp of Midian spread right beneath them. That night came the Divine command to Gideon to go down to the camp, for God had given it into his hand. And yet, alike in condescension to Gideon's weakness, and to show how thoroughly the Lord had prepared the victory, He first allowed him to ascertain for himself the state of matters in the camp of Midian. Quietly Gideon and his page *Phurah* ("the branch") crept from rock to rock, over where the last patrol of the advance-guard[2] kept watch around the camp-fire. Here they overheard the tale of a strange dream. Alike the dream and its interpretation are peculiarly Eastern and in character. Both would make the deepest impression on those sons of the desert, and, communicated to the next patrol, as the first watch was relieved by the second, must have prepared for that panic which, commencing with the advance-guard, was so soon to spread through the whole camp of Midian. The dream was simply this: "Behold, a loaf of barley-bread rolled itself into the camp of Midian, and it came to the tent (the principal one, that of the general), and struck it, and it fell, and it turned from above[3] —and it was fallen!" To which his neighbour (comrade) replied: "This is nothing else but the sword of Gideon, the son of Joash, a man of Israel; given hath the God[4] into his hand Midian and all his camp." So wondrous seemed the dream and its interpretation, that, when Gideon and his armour-bearer heard it, they bent in silent worship, assuredly knowing that God had given them the victory. In truth, with the tale of this dream the miracle of the victory had already begun.

[1] So we understand the expression: "And the camp of Midian was beneath him in the valley."

[2] Judges vii. 11: "The end of the advance-guard;" the latter seems to be the meaning of *Chamushim*. See Josh. i. 14.

[3] So that the upper part was downwards.

[4] "The Elohim," emphatically, with the article.

There is such pictorialness and such truthfulness of detail about all this narrative, that we almost seem to see the events enacted before us. That camp of Bedouins, like locusts in number—with their wives, children, and camels, like the sand by the seashore; then the watchfire by which alone they keep guard; the talk over the camp-fire; the dream so peculiarly Bedouin, and its rapid interpretation, no less characteristically Eastern—and yet the while all ordered and arranged of God—while that small band of three hundred Israelites lies concealed on the neighbouring height, and Gideon and his "young man," are close by, behind the great shadows which the watch-fire casts, hidden perhaps in the long grass! Then the dream itself! It was all quite natural, and yet most unnatural. The Midianites—especially the advanced-guard, that lay nearest to Israel, could not be ignorant that Gideon and his host occupied yonder height. Fame would spread, probably exaggerate, the "mighty valour" of Gideon, and the valour of his followers—while the diminished numbers of Gideon would, of course, not be known, as they had retired by circuitous routes. Moreover, the Midianites must also have been aware that this was to Israel a religious war; nor can they have been ignorant of the might of Jehovah. The fears which all this inspired appear in the interpretation of the dream. But the dream itself was the result of the same feelings. Barley-bread was deemed the poorest food; yet a loaf of this despised provision of slaves rolls itself into Midian's camp, strikes the tent of the leader, turns it upside down, and it falls! Here is a dream-picture of Israel and its victory—all quite natural, yet marvellously dreamed and told just at that peculiar time. And still, often do dreams, excited by natural causes, link themselves, in God's appointment, to thoughts that come supernaturally. We have throughout this history marked how often what seemed to happen quite naturally, was used by God miraculously, and how the supernatural linked itself to what, more or less, had its counterpart in the ordinary course of nature. It had been so in the history of Moses and of Israel; it was so when Joshua defeated the allied kings before Gibeon, and when Barak encountered the invincible chariots of Sisera. In each case it was the Lord, Who gave miraculous victory through terrific tempest. So also it had been in an hour, when thoughts of Israel's past and present must have burned deepest into the heart of Gideon, that the Angel stood before him, even as it was by means most natural that God separated from the rest the three hundred who had not bent the knee to Baal, and who alone were to go to the holy war. Thoughts like these do not detract from, they only make the supernatural the more marvellous. Yet they seem also to bring it nearer to us, till we feel ourselves likewise within its circle, and can realise that even our "daily bread" comes to us straight from heaven!

Gideon and Phurah have returned to the waiting host. In whispered words he has told what they had witnessed. And now the three hundred are divided into three companies. It is not the naked sword they grasp, for in that night not Israel, but Jehovah is to fight. In one hand each man holds a trumpet, in the other, concealed in a pitcher, a burning torch. Each is to do exactly as the leader. Silently they creep round to three different parts of Midian's camp. The guard has just been relieved, and the new watchers have settled quietly by the watch-fire. Suddenly a single trumpet is heard, then three hundred—here, there, everywhere the sound of war is raised. The night is peopled with terrors. Now with loud crash three hundred pitchers are broken; three hundred torches flash through the darkness; three hundred voices shout: "The sword for Jehovah and for Gideon!" Then is the enemy all around the camp! No one can say in what numbers. Again and again rings the trumpet-sound; wave the torches. The camp is roused. Men, women, children, camels rush terror-stricken through the dark night. No one knows but that the enemy is in the very midst of them, and that the neighbour whom he meets is an Israelite, for all around still sounds the war-trumpet, flash the torches, and rises the war-cry. Each man's sword is turned against his neighbour. Mu'titudes are killed or trampled down, and their cries and groans increase the terror of that wild night. A hopeless panic ensues, and ere morning-light, the site of the camp and the road of the fugitives towards Jordan are strewed with the slain.[1]

CHAPTER XVII.

Farther Course of Gideon—The Ephod at Ophrah—Death of Gideon—Conspiracy of Abimelech—The Parable of Jotham—Rule and End of Abimelech.

(JUDGES VII. 23–IX.)

THE tide of battle had rolled towards the Jordan. The fugitives seem to have divided into two main bodies. The quickest, under the leadership of Zebah and Zalmunna, succeeded in crossing the Jordan, and hastened towards the wilderness, while the main body of the army, encumbered with women and cattle, fled in a south-easterly direction, trying to gain the more southern fords of the Jordan within the possession of Issachar, and almost in a straight line with that of Ephraim. The two kings were the object of Gideon's own pursuit, in which he was joined by those of Naphtali, Asher, and Manasseh, who had shortly before been dismissed from the battle. To overtake the other body of fugitives, Gideon summoned the Ephraimites, directing them to occupy "the waters," or tributaries of Jordan, unto Beth-barah (the house of springs) and the Jordan. The success of Ephraim was complete. A great battle seems to have been fought (Is. x. 26), in which the leaders of the Midianites, Oreb and Zeeb ("the raven" and "the wolf") were taken and slain. The Ephraimites continued the pursuit of the fugitives to the other side of the Jordan,

---

[1] It is interesting to notice, that both classical and modern history record similar night-surprises, with ensuing panic and slaughter, though, of course, not of the miraculous character of this narrative.

bringing with them to Gideon the gory heads of Oreb and Zeeb. Strange and sad, that their first meeting with Gideon after this victory should have been one of reproaches and strife, on account of their not having been first summoned to the war—strife, springing from that tribal jealousy which influenced for such evil the whole history of Ephraim. Nor was the reply of Gideon much more satisfactory than their noisy self-assertion (viii. 1–3). To us at least it savours more of the diplomacy of an Oriental, than the straightforward bearing of the warrior of God.

While Ephraim occupied "the waters" and the fords of the Jordan, Gideon himself had crossed the river at the spot where Jacob of old had entered Canaan on his return from Padan-Aram. "Faint yet pursuing," the band reached *Succoth;* but its "princes" refused even the most useful provisions to Gideon's men. The people of the neighbouring Penuel acted in the same heartless manner—no doubt from utter lack of interest in the cause of God, from cowardice, and, above all, from scorn for the small band of 300, with which Gideon had gone in pursuit of the flower of Midian's army. They had calculated the result by the outward means employed, but were destined soon to feel the consequences of their folly. Making a detour eastwards, through the wilderness, Gideon advanced on the rear of Midian, and fell unexpectedly upon the camp at Karkor, which was held by 15,000 men under the command of Zebah and Zalmunna ("sacrifice" and "protection refused"). The surprise ended in defeat and flight, the two Midianite leaders being made prisoners and taken across Jordan. On his way,[1] Gideon "taught the men of Succoth," by punishing their rulers[2]—seventy-seven in number, probably consisting of either seven,

---

[1] In Judges viii. 13 the rendering should be, "from the ascent of Heres," probably a mountain-road by which he came—instead of "before the sun was up."

[2] The notice in viii. 14 (literally rendered), that the lad "wrote down for him" the names of the princes, is interesting as showing the state of education at the time even in so remote a district.

or else five "princes," and of seventy or else seventy-two elders—while in the case of Penuel, which seems to have offered armed resistance to the destruction of its citadel, "the men of the city" were actually slain.

The fate of Gideon's princely captives did not long remain doubtful. It seems that he would have spared their lives, if they had not personally taken part in the slaughter of his brothers, which may have occurred at the commencement of the last campaign, and while the Midianites held Jezreel—possibly under circumstances of treachery and cruelty, prompted perhaps by tidings that Gideon had raised the standard of resistance. It may have been to investigate the facts on the spot, that Gideon had brought back [1] the two princes, or he may have only heard of it on his return. At any rate, the two Midianites not only confessed, but boasted of their achievement. By the law of retaliation they were now made to suffer death, although the hesitation of Gideon's son spared them the humiliation of falling by the hand of a young lad.

The deliverance of Israel was now complete. It had been wrought most unexpectedly, and by apparently quite inadequate means. In the circumstances, it was natural that, in measure as the people failed to recognise the direct agency of Jehovah, they should exalt Gideon as the great national hero. Accordingly, they now offered him the hereditary rule over, at least, the northern tribes. Gideon had spiritual discernment and strength sufficient to resist this temptation. He knew that he had only been called to a temporary work, and that the "rule" which they wished could not be made hereditary. Each "judge" must be specially called, and qualified by the influence of the Holy Spirit. Besides, the latter was not, as since the ascension of our Blessed Saviour, a permanent indwelling of the Holy Spirit as a Person, but consisted in certain effects produced by His agency. The proposal of Israel could therefore only arise from carnal misunderstanding, and must be refused.

---

[1] We gather that this took place either in Jezreel or at Ophrah from the circumstance that Gideon's son had joined him: viii. 20.

But Gideon himself was not proof against another temptation and mistake. God had called him not only to temporal, but to spiritual deliverance of Israel. He had thrown down the altar of Baal; he had built up that of Jehovah, and offered on it accepted sacrifice. Shiloh was deserted, and the high priest seemed set aside. Ophrah had been made what Shiloh should have been, and Gideon had taken the place of the high priest. All this had been by express Divine command—and without any reference to the services of the tabernacle. Moreover, Gideon's office had never been recalled. Should it not now be made permanent, at least, in his own person? The keeping of Israel's faith had been committed to his strong hand; should he deliver it up to the feeble grasp of a nominal priesthood which had proved itself incapable of such a trust? It was to this temptation that Gideon succumbed. when he asked of the people the various golden ornaments, taken as spoil from the enemy.[1] The gold so obtained amounted to seventeen thousand shekels—or nearly the weight of fifty pounds. With this Gideon made an ephod, no doubt with the addition of the high-priestly breastplate and its precious gems, and of the Urim and Thummim. Here, then, was the commencement of a spurious worship. Presently, Israel went to Ophrah, " a whoring after it," while to Gideon himself and to his house this "thing became a snare."[2]

In truth, the same spiritual misunderstanding which culminated in Gideon's arrogating to himself high-priestly functions, had appeared almost immediately after that night-victory of Jehovah over Midian. Even his reply to the jealous wrangling of Ephraim does not sound like the straightforward language of one who had dismissed the thousands of Israel to go to

---

[1] It is well known that the Midianites delighted in that kind of ornaments. We recognise in this, even to the present day, the habits of the Bedawîn. If we bear in mind that the host of Midian consisted of 150,000 men, the weight of gold will by no means appear excessive.

[2] The Rabbis find here tribal jealousies against Ephraim, within whose territory were Shiloh and the tabernacle.

battle with only three hundred. Again, there is what at least looks like petty revenge about his dealings with Succoth and Penuel; while it is difficult to understand upon what principle, other than that of personal retaliation, he had made the lives of Zebah and Zalmunna wholly dependent upon their conduct towards his own family. And the brief remarks of Scripture about the family-life of Gideon, after he had made the ephod, only tend to confirm our impressions. But, meantime, for "forty years in the days of Gideon," "the country was in quietness," and, however imperfect in its character, the service of Jehovah seems to have been, at least outwardly, the only one professed. Matters changed immediately upon his death. Presently the worship of Baalim becomes again common, and especially that of the "Covenant-Baal" (Baal-berith). There is a sad lesson here. If Gideon had made a spurious ephod, his people now chose a false "covenant-god." And, having first forsaken the Covenant-Jehovah, they next turned in ingratitude from their earthly deliverer, "neither showed they kindness to the house of Jerubbaal." Thus sin ever brings its own punishment.

Not far from Ophrah, but in the territory of Ephraim, was the ancient *Shechem*, connected with so much that was most solemn in the history of Israel. We know the long-standing tribal jealousy of Ephraim and their desire for leadership. Moreover, as we learn from Judges ix. 28, Shechem seems to have retained among its inhabitants the lineal representatives of Hamor, the original "prince" and founder of Shechem in the days of Jacob (Gen. xxxiii. 19; xxxiv. 2; comp. Josh. xxiv. 32). These would represent, so as speak, the ancient feudal heathen aristocracy of the place, and, of course, the original worshippers of Baal. As perhaps the most ancient city in that part of the country, and as the seat of the descendants of Hamor, Shechem seems to have become the centre of Baal worship. Accordingly we find there the temple of the "Covenant-Baal" (Judges ix. 4). Possibly the latter may have been intended to express and perpetuate the union of the original heathen with the more modern Israelitish, or "Shechem" part of the population. Here then were sufficient elements of mischief ready: tribal jealousy; envy of the great and ancient Shechem towards little Ophrah; hatred of the rule of the house of Gideon; but, above all, the opposition of heathenism. It is very characteristic of this last, as the chief motive at work, that throughout all the intrigues against the house of Gideon, he is never designated by his own name, but always as *Jerubbaal*—he that contended against Baal. Contending against Baal had been the origin of Gideon's power; and to the heathen mind it seemed still embodied in that Jehovah-Ephod in the possession of Gideon's sons at Ophrah. The present rising would in turn be the contending of Baal against the house of Gideon, and his triumph its destruction. It only needed a leader. Considering the authority which the family of Gideon must still have possessed, none better could have been found than one of its own members.

Gideon had left no fewer than seventy sons. If we may judge from their connivance at the worship of Baal around, from the want of any recognised outstanding individuality among them, and especially from their utter inability to make a stand even for life against an equal number of enemies, they must have sadly degenerated; probably were an enervated, luxurious, utterly feeble race. There was one exception, however, to this; one outside their circle, and yet of it—Abimelech, not a legitimate son of Gideon's, but one by " a maidservant," a native of Shechem. Although we know not the possible peculiarities of the case, it is, in general, quite consistent with social relations in the East, that Abimelech's slave-mother should have had influential connections in Shechem, who, although of an inferior grade,[1] could enter into dealings with " the citizens " of the place. Abimelech seems to have

---

[1] This appears from the whole account of their transactions, in which the others are always designated as "lords" of Shechem, in our Authorised Version, "men of Shechem," or rather, probably, the citizens—what we would call the "house-owners" of Shechem.

possessed all the courage, vigour, and energy of his father; only coupled, alas! with restless ambition, reckless unscrupulousness, and daring impiety. His real name we do not know;[1] for *Abimelech*, father-king, or else king-father, seems to have been a by-name, probably suggested by his natural qualifications and his ambition. The plot was well contrived by Abimelech. At his instigation his mother's relatives entered into negotiations with the "citizens" or "householders" of Shechem. The main considerations brought to bear upon them seem to have been: hatred of the house of Gideon, and the fact that Abimelech was a fellow-townsman. This was sufficient. The compact was worthily ratified with Baal's money. Out of the treasury of his temple they gave Abimelech seventy shekels. This wretched sum, somewhere at the rate of half-a-crown a person, sufficed to hire a band of seventy reckless rabble for the murder of Gideon's sons. Such was the value which Israel put upon them! Apparently unresisting, they were all slaughtered upon one stone, like a sacrifice—all but one, Jotham ("Jehovah [is] perfect"), who succeeded in hiding himself, and thus escaped.

This is the first scene. The next brings us once more to "the memorial by the vale"[2] which Joshua had set up, when, at the close of his last address, the people had renewed their covenant with Jehovah (Josh. xxiv. 26, 27). It was in this sacred spot that "the citizens of Shechem and the whole house of Millo"[3] were now gathered to make Abimelech king! Close by, behind it, to the south, rose Gerizim, the Mount of Blessings. On one of its escarpments, which tower 800 feet above the valley, Jotham, the last survivor of Gideon's house, watched the scene. And now his voice rose above the shouts

---

[1] This is rightly inferred by Keil from the meaning of the verb, insufficiently rendered in our Authorised Version: "whose name he called Abimelech" (viii. 31).

[2] Wrongly rendered in our version "by the plain of the pillar," ix. 6.

[3] That is, the inhabitants of Millo. Millo was no doubt the castle or citadel close to Shechem.

of the people. In that clear atmosphere every word made its way to the listeners below. It was a strange parable he told, peculiarly of the East, that land of parables, and in language so clear and forcible, that it stands almost unique. It is about the Republic of Trees, who are about to elect a king. In turn the olive, the fig tree, and the vine, the three great representatives of fruit-bearing trees in Palestine,[1] are asked. But each refuses; for each has its own usefulness, and inquires with wonder: "Am I then to lose" my fatness, or my sweetness, or my wine, "and to go to flutter above the trees?"[2] The expressions are very pictorial, as indicating, on the one hand, that such a reign could only be one of unrest and insecurity, a "wavering" or "fluttering" above the trees, and that, in order to attain this position of elevation above the other trees, a tree would require to be uprooted from its own soil, and so lose what of fatness, sweetness, or refreshment God had intended it to yield. Then, these noble trees having declined the offer, and apparently all the others also,[3] the whole of the trees next turn to the thornbush, which yields no fruit, can give no shadow, and only wounds those who take hold of it, which, in fact, is only fit for burning. The thornbush itself seems scarcely to believe that such a proposal could seriously be made to it. "If in truth" (that is, "truly and sincerely") "ye anoint me king over you, come, put your trust in my shadow;[4] but if not (that is, if you fear so to do, or else find your hopes disappointed), let fire come out of the thornbush and devour the cedars of Lebanon."[5] The application of the parable was so evident,

[1] The Rabbis understand the three trees as referring to Othniel, Deborah, and Gideon.
[2] So literally.
[3] This we gather from the fact that "the trees" successively solicit the olive, the fig, and the vine, while afterwards "*all* the trees" are said to turn to the thorn, as if all of them had been successively asked, and had declined.
[4] Seek shelter under my shadow.
[5] That is, the noblest and the best. The thorn is easily set on fire—indeed, fit for nothing else.

that it scarcely needed the pungent sentences in which Jotham in conclusion set before the people their conduct in its real character.

Jotham had not spoken as a prophet, but his language was prophetic. Three years, not of kingdom, but of rule,[1] and the judgment of God, which had been slumbering, began to descend. Scripture marks distinctly both the Divine agency in the altered feeling of Shechem towards Abimelech, and its import as boding judgment. The course of events is vividly sketched. First, the citizens post "liers in wait" in all the mountain passes, in the vain hope of seizing Abimelech. The consequence is universal brigandage. This device having failed, they next invite, or at least encourage the arrival among them of a freebooting adventurer with his band. It is the season of vintage, and, strange and terrible as it may sound, a service, specially ordered by Jehovah, is observed, but only to be prostituted to Baal. According to Lev. xix. 24, the produce of the fourth year's fruit planting was to be brought as "praise-offerings" (*Hillulim*) to Jehovah. And now these men of Shechem "made praise offerings"[2] (Hillulim), but went with them into the house of Baal-berith. At the sacrificial feast which followed, wine soon loosened the tongues. It is an appeal to Baal as against the house of Jerubbaal; a revolt of old Shechem against modern Shechem; in favour of the old patrician descendants of Hamor against Abimelech and his lieutenant Zebul.[3] This insulting challenge, addressed in true Oriental fashion to the absent, is conveyed by secret messengers

---

[1] The expression in ix. 22 is *not* that Abimelech reigned as a king, but that he lorded it.

[2] Our Authorised Version translates wrongly ix. 27 : "And they went out into the fields, ... and made merry." This last clause should be rendered, "and made *Hillulim*—praise offerings."

[3] The language is very pictorial in its contrast of young Shechem with old Shechem, or rather Hamor ; and in laying emphasis upon the name Jerubbaal. The challenge to Abimelech is, of course, not to be regarded as delivered to himself, but, as so common in the East, addressed to an imaginary Abimelech.

to Abimelech.[1] That night he and his band move forward. Divided into four companies, they occupy all the heights around Shechem. Ignorant how near was danger, Gaal stands next morning in the gate with his band, in the same spirit of boastfulness as at the festival of the previous night. He is still, as it were, challenging imaginary foes. Zebul is also there. As Abimelech's men are seen moving down towards the valley, Zebul first tries to lull Gaal's suspicions. And now they are appearing in all directions—from the mountains, "from the heights of the land," and one company "from the way of the terebinth of the magicians."[2] Zebul now challenges Gaal to make good his boasting. A fight ensues in view of the citizens of Shechem, in which Gaal and his band are discomfited, and he and his adherents are finally expelled from the town. If the Shechemites had thought thus to purchase immunity, they were speedily undeceived. Abimelech was hovering in the neighbourhood, and, when the unsuspecting people were busy in their fields, he surprised and slaughtered them, at the same time occupying the city, which was razed to the ground and sowed with salt. Upon this the citizens of the tower, or of Millo, sought refuge in the sacred precincts of "the hall of the god Berith." But in vain. Abimelech set it on fire, and 1000 persons perished in the flames. Even this did not satisfy his revenge. He next turned his forces against the neighbouring town of Thebez. Reduced to the utmost straits, its inhabitants fled to the strong tower within the city. Thither Abimelech pursued them. Almost had the people of Thebez shared the fate of the citizens of Millo, when Abimelech's course was strangely arrested. From the top of the tower a woman cast down upon him an "upper millstone."[3] As the Rabbis put it, he, that had slaughtered his brothers upon a stone, was killed

---

[1] The message of Zebul (ix. 31) was: "they raise the city against thee," viz., in rebellion—not, as in our Authorised Version, "they fortify the city against thee."

[2] In the Authorised Version (ver. 37) "the plain of the Meonenim."

[3] In the Authorised Version (ver. 53) "a piece of a millstone."

by a stone. Abimelech died as he had lived. Feeling himself mortally wounded, ambitious warrior to the last, he had himself run through by the sword of his armour-bearer, to avoid the disgrace of perishing by the hand of a woman. But his epitaph, and that of the men of Shechem who had perished by his hand, had been long before written in the curse of Jotham.

CHAPTER XVIII.

Successors of Abimelech—Chronology of the Period—Israel's renewed Apostacy, and their Humiliation before Jehovah—Oppression by the Ammonites—Jephthah—His History and Vow—The Successors of Jephthah.

(JUDGES X.–XII.)

THE sudden and tragic end of Abimelech seems to have awakened repentance among the people. It is thus that we explain the mention of his name (x. 1) in connection with three judges, who successively ruled over the northern tribes. The first of these was *Tola* (" scarlet-worm "),[1] the son of *Puah* (probably " red dye ") and grandson of Dodo, a man of Issachar. His reign lasted twenty-three years, and was followed by that of *Jair* (" Enlightener "), who judged twenty-two years. The family notice of the latter indicates great influence, each of his thirty sons appearing as a " chief " (riding on " ass-colts "), and their property extending over thirty out of the sixty cities (1 Kings iv. 13; 1 Chron. ii. 23) which formed the ancient Havoth-Jair, or circuits of Jair[2] (Numb. xxxii. 41; Deut. iii. 14).

[1] Some have translated this by the son of "his uncle," viz., the uncle of Abimelech. But this seems unlikely, as Gideon was of Manasseh, and Tola of Issachar. The names of *Tola* and *Puah*, or Phuvah (Gen. xlvi. 13; Numb. xxvi. 23), as well as that of *Jair*, were *tribal* names.

[2] Certain critics have imagined a discrepancy between the earlier notice

These forty-five years of comparative rest conclude the second period in the history of the Judges. The third, which commences with fresh apostacy on the part of Israel, includes the contemporaneous rule of *Jephthah* and his successors—Ibzan, Elon, and Abdon (xii. 8-15)—in the north and east, and of *Samson* in the south and west. While in the north and east Jephthah encountered the Ammonites, Samson warred against the Philistines in the south-west. The oppression of Ammon over the eastern and northern tribes lasted eighteen years (x. 8, 9); the rule of Jephthah six years (xii. 7); that of his three successors twenty-five years—covering in all a period of forty-nine years. On the other hand, the oppression of the Philistines lasted in all forty years (xiii. 1), during twenty years of which (xv. 20) Samson "began to deliver Israel" (xiii. 5), the deliverance being completed only twenty years later under Samuel, when the battle of Ebenezer was gained (1 Sam. vii.). Thus Abdon, Jephthah's last successor in the north, must have died nine years after the battle of Ebenezer. These dates are of great importance, not only on their own account, but because they show us the two parallel streams of Israel's history in the north and the south. Again, the coincidence of events in the south with those in the north casts fresh light upon both. Thus, as Eli's high-priestly administration, which in a general sense is designated as "judging Israel," lasted forty years (1 Sam. iv. 18), and his death took place about twenty years and seven months before the victory of Samuel over the Philistines (1 Sam. vi. 1; vii. 2), it is evident that the first twenty years of Eli's administration were contemporary with that of Jair in the east, while the last twenty were marked by the Philistine oppression, which continued forty years. In that case Samson must

---

in Numb. xxxii. **41**, etc., and that in the text. But the text does *not* say that the Havoth-Jair obtained its name in the period of the Judges—rather the opposite, as will appear from the following rendering of Judges x. 4: " and they had thirty cities (of) those which are called the circuit of Jair *even* unto this day."

have been born, and have grown up during the high priesthood of Eli, and most of his exploits, as judging Israel for twenty years, taken place under Samuel, who gained the battle of Ebenezer, and so put an end to Philistine oppression, a short time after the death of Samson. In connection with this we may note, that Samuel's period of judging is only mentioned *after* the battle of Ebenezer (1 Sam. vii. 15).

There is another and very important fact to be considered. The terrible fate which overtook the house of Gideon, culminating in the death of Abimelech, seems for ever to have put an end to the spurious ephod-worship of Jehovah, or to that in any other place than that He had chosen, or through any other than the Levitical priesthood. *Accordingly, the sanctuary of Shiloh and its ministers now come again, and permanently, into prominent notice.* This not only in the case of Eli and Samuel, but long before that. This appears from the sacred text. For when, previous to the calling of Jephthah, the children of Israel repented, we are told that they "cried unto the Lord," and that the Lord spake unto them, to which they in turn made suitable reply (Judges x. 10, 11, 15). But the peculiar expressions used leave no doubt on our mind, that the gathering of Israel before the Lord had taken place in His sanctuary at Shiloh, and the answer of Jehovah been made by means of the Urim and Thummim (comp. Judges i. 1).

For clearness' sake, it may be well to explain, that Judges x. 6–18 forms a general introduction, alike to the history of Jephthah and his successors, and to that of Samson. In ver. 6 *seven* national deities are mentioned whom Israel had served, besides the Baalim and Ashtaroth of Canaan. This in opposition to the *sevenfold* deliverance (vers. 11, 12) which Israel had experienced at the hands of Jehovah.[1] Then

---

[1] Israel's unfaithfulness is represented as keeping measure, so to speak, with God's mercy and deliverance. The significance of the number seven should not be overlooked. Instead of "the Maonites" in ver. 12 the LXX. read "Midianites," which seems the more correct reading. Otherwise it must refer to the tribe mentioned 2 Chron. xxvi. 7; comp. 1 Chron. iv. 41.

follows, in ver. 7, a general reference to the twofold contemporaneous oppression by the Ammonites in the east and north, and by the Philistines in the south and west. In ver. 8 the account of the Ammonites' oppression[1] commences with the statement, that "they ground down and bruised the children of Israel that year," and in a similar manner for eighteen years. In fact, the Ammonites, in their successful raids across the Jordan, occupied districts of the territory of Judah, Benjamin, and Ephraim, which bordered either on the Dead Sea or on the fords of Jordan.[2] Next, we have in verses 10–15 an account of Israel's humiliation and entreaty at Shiloh, and of the Lord's answer by the Urim and Thummim. Finally, ver. 16 informs us, how the genuineness of their repentance appeared not in professions and promises, but in the putting away of all "strange gods," and that when there was no immediate prospect of Divine help. After this, to reproduce the wonderful imagery of Scripture: "His soul became short on account of the misery of Israel." That misery had lasted too long; He could not, as it were, be any longer angry with them, nor bear to see their suffering. For, as a German writer beautifully observes: "The love of God is not like the hard and fast logical sequences of man; it is ever free. . . . The parable of the prodigal affords a glimpse of the marvellous 'inconsistency' of the Father, who receives the wanderer when he suffered the consequences of his sin. . . . Put away the strange gods, and the withered rod will burst anew into life and verdure." And such is ever God's love—full and free. For, in the words of the author just quoted: "Sin and forgiveness are the pivots of all history, specially of that of Israel, including in that term the spiritual Israel."

Now, indeed, was deliverance at hand. For the first time these eighteen years that Ammon had camped in Gilead, the children of Israel also camped against them in Mizpeh, or, as it is

---

[1] That of the Philistines commences xiii. 1.

[2] I do not suppose that the Ammonites traversed the land, but that they made raids across the fords of Jordan, and laid waste the contiguous districts.

otherwise called (Josh. xiii. 26 ; xx. 8), in Ramath-Mizpeh or Ramoth-Gilead (the modern *Salt*), a city east of the Jordan, in an almost direct line from Shiloh. The camp of Israel could not have been better chosen. Defended on three sides by high hills, Mizpeh lay "on two sides of a narrow ravine, half way up, crowned by a (now) ruined citadel,"[1] which probably at all times defended the city. "Ramoth-Gilead must always have been the key of Gilead, at the head of the only easy road from the Jordan, opening immediately on to the rich plateau of the interior, and with this isolated cone rising close above it, fortified from very early times, by art as well as by nature." All was thus prepared, and now the people of Gilead, through their "princes," resolved to offer the supreme command to any one who had already begun to fight against the children of Ammon—that is, who on his own account had waged warfare, and proved successful against them. This notice is of great importance for the early history of Jephthah.

Few finer or nobler characters are sketched even in Holy Scripture than *Jephthah*, or rather Jiphthach ("the breaker through"). He is introduced to us as "a mighty man of valour"—the same terms in which the angel had first addressed Gideon (vi. 12). But this "hero of might" must first learn to conquer his own spirit. His history is almost a parallel to that of Abimelech—only in the way of *contrast*. For, whereas Abimelech had of his own accord left his father's house to plan treason, Jephthah was wrongfully driven out by his brothers from his father's inheritance. Abimelech had appealed to the citizens of Shechem to help him in his abominable ambition; Jephthah to the "elders of Gilead" for redress in his wrong, but apparently in vain (xi. 7). Abimelech had committed unprovoked and cruel murder with his hired band; Jephthah withdrew to the land of *Tob*, which, from 2 Sam. x. 6, 8, we know to have been on the northern boundary of Peræa, between Syria and the land of Ammon. There he gathered

---

[1] The description is taken from Canon Tristram's *Land of Israel*, pp. 557, 560.

around him a number of freebooters, as David afterwards in similar circumstances (1 Sam. xxii. 2); not, like Abimelech, to destroy his father's house, but, like David, to war against the common foe. This we infer from Judges x. 18, which shows that, before the war between Gilead and Ammon, Jephthah had acquired fame as contending against Ammon. This life of adventure would suit the brave Gileadite and his followers; for he was a wild mountaineer, only imbued with the true spirit of Israel. And now, when war had actually broken out, " the elders of Gilead " were not in doubt whom to choose as their chief. They had seen and repented their sin against Jehovah, and now they saw and confessed their wrong towards Jephthah, and appealed to his generosity. In ordinary circumstances he would not have consented; but he came back to them, as the elders of Gilead had put it, because they were in distress. Nor did he come in his own strength. The agreement made with the elders of Israel was solemnly ratified before Jehovah.

He that has a righteous cause will not shrink from having it thoroughly sifted. It was not because Jephthah feared the battle, but because he wished to avoid bloodshed, that he twice sent an embassy of remonstrance to the king of Ammon. The claims of the latter upon the land between the Arnon and the Jabbok were certainly of the most shadowy kind. That country had, at the time of the Israelitish conquest, belonged to Sihon, king of the Amorites. True, the Amorites were not its original owners, having wrested the land from Moab (Numb. xxi. 26). Balak might therefore have raised a claim; but, although he hired Balaam to protect what still remained of his kingdom against a possible attack by Israel, which he dreaded, he never attempted to recover what Israel had taken from the Amorites, although it had originally been his. Moreover, even in dealing with the Amorites, as before with Edom and Moab, whose territory Israel had actually avoided by a long circuit, the utmost forbearance had been shown. If the Amorites had been dispossessed, theirs had been the unprovoked attack, when Israel had in the first place only asked a passage through their country. Lastly, if 300 years'[1] undisputed possession of the land did not give a prescriptive right, it would be difficult to imagine by what title land could be held. Nor did Jephthah shrink from putting the matter on its ultimate and best ground. Addressing the Ammonites, as from their religious point of view they could understand it, he said: "And now Jehovah God of Israel hath dispossessed the Amorites from before His people, and shouldest thou possess it? Is it not so, that which Chemosh[2] thy god giveth thee to possess, that wilt thou possess; and all that which Jehovah our God shall dispossess before us, that shall we possess?" We do not wonder that of a war commenced in such a spirit we should be told: "And the Spirit of the Lord came upon Jephthah." Presently Jephthah passed all through the land east of the Jordan, and its people obeyed his summons.

We are now approaching what to many will appear the most difficult part in the history of Jephthah—perhaps among the most difficult narratives in the Bible. It appears that, before actually going to war, Jephthah solemnly registered this vow: "If thou indeed givest the children of Ammon into mine hand—and it shall be, the outcoming (one), that shall come out from the door of my house to meet me on my returning in peace from the children of Ammon, shall be to Jehovah, and I will offer that a burnt offering." We know that the vow *was* paid. The defeat of the Ammonites was thorough and crushing. But on Jephthah's return to his house the first to welcome him was his only daughter—his only child—who at the head of the maidens came to greet the victor. There is a terrible irony about those "timbrels and dances," with which Jephthah's daughter went, as it were, to celebrate her own funeral obsequies, while the fond father's heart was well-nigh breaking. But the

---

[1] Of course these are round numbers, and not to be regarded as strictly arithmetical.

[2] *Chemosh*—the destroyer or desolater—the Moabite god of war. He is represented on coins with a sword in his right hand, a spear and lance in his left; the figure being flanked by burning torches.

noble maiden was the first to urge his observance of the vow unto Jehovah. Only two months did she ask to bewail her maidenhood with her companions upon the mountains. But ever after was it a custom for the maidens in Israel to go out every year for four days, "to praise[1] the daughter of Jephthah."

Such is the story; but what is its meaning? What did Jephthah really intend by the language of his vow; and did he feel himself bound by it in the literal sense to offer up his daughter as a burnt sacrifice? Assuredly, we shall make no attempt either to explain away the facts of the case, or to disguise the importance of the questions at issue. At the outset we are here met by these two facts: that up to that period Jephthah had both acted and spoken as a true worshipper of Jehovah, and that his name stands emblazoned in that roll of the heroes of the faith which is handed down to us in the Epistle to the Hebrews (xi. 32). But it is well-nigh impossible to believe that a true worshipper of Jehovah could have either vowed or actually offered a human sacrifice—not to speak of the sacrifice being that of his own and only child. Such sacrifices were the most abhorrent and opposed to the whole spirit and letter of the Law of God (Lev. xviii. 21; xx. 2–5; Deut. xii. 31; xviii. 10), nor do we find any mention of them till the reigns of the wicked Ahaz and Manasseh. Not even Jezebel had ventured to introduce them; and we know what thrill of horror ran through the onlookers, when the *heathen* king of Moab offered his son an expiatory sacrifice on the walls of his capital (2 Kings iii. 26, etc.). But the difficulty becomes well-

---

[1] This is the correct rendering, and not "lament," as in our Authorised Version. There was a curious custom in Israel in the days of our Lord. Twice in the year, "on the 15th of Ab, when the collection of wood for the sanctuary was completed, and on the Day of Atonement, the maidens of Jerusalem went in white garments, specially lent them for the purpose, so that rich and poor might be on an equality, into the vineyards close to the city, where they danced and sung" (see my *Temple: its Services and Ministry at the time of Jesus Christ*, p. 286). Could this strange practice have been a remnant of the maidens' praise of the daughter of Jephthah?

nigh insuperable, when we find the name of Jephthah recorded in the New Testament among the heroes of the faith. Surely, no one guilty of such a crime could have found a place there! Still, these are considerations which, though most important, are outside the narrative itself, and in any truthful investigation the latter should, in the first place, be studied by itself.

In so doing we must dismiss, as irrelevant and untruthful, such pleas as the roughness of those times, the imperfectness of religious development, or that of religious ignorance on the part of the outlaw Jephthah, who had spent most of his life far from Israel. The Scripture sketch of Jephthah leaves, indeed, on the mind the impression of a genuine, wild, and daring Gilead mountaineer—a sort of warrior-Elijah. But, on the other hand, he acts and speaks throughout as a true worshipper of Jehovah. And his vow, which in the Old Testament always expresses the highest religious feeling (Gen. xxviii. 20; 1 Sam. i. 11; Ps. cxvi. 14; Is. xix. 21), is so sacred *because* it is made to Jehovah. Again, in his embassy to the king of Ammon, Jephthah displays the most intimate acquaintance with the Pentateuch, his language being repeatedly almost a literal quotation from Numb. xx. He who knew so well the details of Scripture history could not have been ignorant of its fundamental principles. Having thus cleared the way, we observe:

1. That the language of Jephthah's vow implied, from the first, at least the possibility of some human being coming out from the door of his house, to meet him on his return. The original conveys this, and the evident probabilities of the case were strongly in favour of such an eventuality. Indeed, Jephthah's language seems to have been designedly chosen in such general terms as to cover all cases. But it is impossible to suppose that Jephthah would have deliberately *made a vow* in which he contemplated human sacrifice; still more so, that Jehovah would have connected victory and deliverance with such a horrible crime.

2. In another particular, also, the language of Jephthah's vow is remarkable. It is, that "the outcoming (whether man or beast) shall be to Jehovah, and I will offer that a burnt-offering." The great Jewish commentators of the Middle Ages have, in opposition to the Talmud, pointed out that these two last clauses are *not* identical. It is never said of an *animal* burnt-offering, that it "shall be to Jehovah"—for the simple reason that, as a burnt-offering, *it is* such. But where human beings are offered to Jehovah, there the expression is used, as in the case of the first-born among Israel and of Levi (Numb. iii. 12, 13). But in these cases it has never been suggested that there was actual human sacrifice.

3. It was a principle of the Mosaic law, that burnt sacrifices were to be exclusively *males* (Lev. i. 3).

4. If the loving daughter had devoted herself to *death*, it is next to incredible that she should have wished to spend the two months of life conceded to her, not with her broken-hearted father, but in the mountains with her companions.

5. She bewails not her "maiden age," but her "maidenhood" —not that she dies so young, but that she is to die unmarried. The Hebrew expression for the former would have been quite different from that used in Scripture, which only signifies the latter.[1] But for an only child to die unmarried, and so to leave a light and name extinguished in Israel, was indeed a bitter and heavy judgment, viewed in the light of pre-Messianic times. Compare in this respect especially such passages as Lev. xx. 20 and Psalm lxxviii. 63. The trial appears all the more withering when we realise, how it must have come upon Jephthah and his only child in the hour of their highest glory, when all earthly prosperity seemed at their command. The greatest and happiest man in Israel becomes in a moment the poorest and the most stricken. Surely, in this vow and sacrifice was the lesson of vows and sacrifices taught to victorious Israel in a manner the most solemn.

---

[1] The Hebrew expression is *bethulim*. If it meant maiden age it would probably, as Keil remarks, have been *neurim* (comp. Lev. xxi. 13).

6. It is very significant that in xi. 39 it is only said, that Jephthah "did with her according to his vow"—not that he actually offered her in sacrifice, while in the latter case the added clause, "and she knew no man," would be utterly needless and unmeaning. *Lastly,* we may ask, Who would have been the priest by whom, and where the altar on which, such a sacrifice could have been offered unto Jehovah?

On all these grounds—its utter contrariety to the whole Old Testament, the known piety of Jephthah, the blessing following upon his vow, his mention in the Epistle to the Hebrews, but especially the language of the narrative itself—we feel bound to reject the idea of any human sacrifice. In what special manner, besides remaining unmarried,[1] the vow of her dedication to God was carried out, we do not feel bound to suggest. Here the principle, long ago expressed by Clericus, holds true: "We are not to imagine that, in so small a volume as the Old Testament, *all* the customs of the Hebrews are recorded, or the full history of all that had taken place among them. Hence there are necessarily allusions to many things which cannot be fully followed out, because there is no mention of them elsewhere."

Yet another trial awaited Jephthah. The tribal jealousy of Ephraim, which treated the Gileadites (more especially the half tribe of Manasseh) as mere runaways from Ephraim, who had no right to independent tribal action, scarcely to independent existence—least of all to having one of their number a "Judge," now burst into a fierce war. Defeated in battle, the Ephraimites tried to escape to the eastern bank of the Jordan; but Gilead had occupied the fords. Their peculiar pronunciation[2] betrayed Ephraim, and a horrible massacre ensued.

---

[1] In general, the Mishnah condemns in unmeasured terms female asceticism (Sotah iii. 4). But in the Talmud (Sotah 22a) one instance at least is recorded with special praise, in which a virgin wholly devoted herself to prayer. See Cassel in *Herzog's Encyclop.* vi. p. 475, note.

[2] *Shibboleth* means stream, which the Ephraimites pronounced Sibboleth

Six years of rest—" then died Jephthah the Gileadite, and was buried in one of the cities of Gilead." We know not the locality, nor yet the precise place where he had lived, nor the city in which his body was laid. No father's home had welcomed him; no child was left to cheer his old age. He lived alone, and he died alone. Truly, as has been remarked, his sorrow and his victory are a type of Him Who said : " Not my will, but Thine be done."

It almost seems as if Jephthah's three successors in the judgeship of the eastern and northern tribes were chiefly mentioned to mark the contrast in their history. Of Ibzan of Bethlehem,[1] of Elon the Zebulonite, and of Abdon the Pirathonite, we know alike the dwelling and the burying-place. They lived honoured, and died blessed—surrounded, as the text emphatically tells us, by a large and prosperous number of descendants. But their names are not found in the catalogue of worthies whom the Holy Ghost has selected for our special example and encouragement.

CHAPTER XIX.

Meaning of the History of Samson—His Annunciation and early History—The Spirit of Jehovah "impels him"—His Deeds of Faith.

(JUDGES XIII.-XV.)

THERE is yet another name recorded in the Epistle to the Hebrews among the Old Testament "worthies," whose title to that position must to many have seemed at least doubtful. Can Samson claim a place among the spiritual

---

[1] The Bethlehem here spoken of is, of course, not that in Judah, but that in Zebulon (Josh. xix. 15). The situation of *Ajalon*, the modern *Salem*, quite in the north of Zebulon, and of *Pirathon* in Ephraim, the modern *Ferata*, six miles west of Nablus, has been ascertained.

heroes, who "through faith subdued kingdoms, wrought righteousness, obtained promises?" The question cannot be dismissed with a summary answer, for if, as we believe, the Holy Spirit pronounced such judgment on his activity as a judge, then careful and truthful study of his history must bear it out. But then also must that history have been commonly misread and misunderstood. Let it be remembered, that it is of Samson's activity as a Judge, and under the impulse of the Spirit of God, we are writing, and *not* of every act of his life. In fact, we shall presently distinguish two periods in his history; the first, when he acted under the influence of that Spirit; the second, when, yielding to his passions, he fell successively into sin, unfaithfulness to his calling, and betrayal of it, followed by the desertion of Jehovah and by His judgment. And, assuredly, the language of the Epistle to the Hebrews could not apply to the period of Samson's God-desertion and of his punishment, but only to that of his first activity or of his later repentance.

It was in the days of Eli the high priest. Strange and tangled times these, when once again principles rather than men were to come to the front, if Israel was to be revived and saved. The period of the Judges had run its course to the end. The result had been general disorganisation, an almost complete disintegration of the tribes, and decay of the sanctuary. But now, just at the close of the old, the new was beginning; or rather, old principles were once more asserted. In Eli the Divine purpose concerning the priesthood, in Samson that concerning the destiny and mission of Israel, were to reappear. In both cases, alike in their strength and in their weakness—in the faithfulness and in the unfaithfulness of its representatives. The whole meaning of Samson's history is, that he was a Nazarite. His strength lay in being a Nazarite; his weakness in yielding to his carnal lusts, and thereby becoming unfaithful to his calling. In both respects he was not only a type of Israel, but, so to speak, a mirror in which Israel could see itself and its history. Israel, the Nazarite people—no achievement, however marvellous, that it could not and did not accomplish! Israel, unfaithful to its vows and yielding to spiritual adultery—no depth of degradation so low, that it would not descend to it! The history of Israel was the history of Samson; his victories were like theirs, till, like him, yielding to the seductions of a Delilah, Israel betrayed and lost its Nazarite strength. And so also with Samson's and with Israel's final repentance and recovery of strength. Viewed in this light, we can not only understand this history, but even its seeming difficulties become so many points of fresh meaning. We can see why his life should have been chronicled with a circumstantiality seemingly out of proportion to the deliverance he wrought; and why there was so little and so transient result of his deeds. When the Spirit of God comes upon him, he does supernatural deeds; not in his own strength, but as a Nazarite, in the strength of God, by Whom and for Whom he had been set apart before his birth. All this showed the meaning and power of the Nazarite; what deliverance God could work for His people even by a single Nazarite, so that, in the language of prophecy, one man could chase a thousand! Thus also we understand the peculiar and almost spasmodic character of Samson's deeds, as also the reason why he always appears on the scene, not at the head of the tribes, but alone to battle.

If the secret of Samson's strength lay in the faithful observance of his Nazarite vow, his weakness sprung from his natural character. The parallel, so far as Israel is concerned, cannot fail to be seen. And as Samson's sin finally assumed the form of adulterous love for Delilah, so that of his people was spiritual unfaithfulness. Thus, if the period of the Judges reached its highest point in Samson the Nazarite, it also sunk to its lowest in Samson the man of carnal lusts, who yielded his secret to a Delilah. As one has put it : " The strength of the Spirit of God bestowed on the Judges for the deliverance of their people was overcome by the power of the flesh lusting against the Spirit." Yet may we, with all reverence, point from Samson, the Nazarite for life,[1] to the great antitype in Jesus

[1] The ordinary Nazarite vow was only for a period. But the later Rabbis

Christ, the "Nazarite among His brethren,"[1] in Whom was fulfilled that "which was spoken by the prophets, He shall be called a Nazarite"[2] (Matt. ii. 23). And it is at any rate remarkable that ancient Jewish tradition, in referring to the blessing spoken to Dan (Gen. xlix. 17, 18), applies this addition: "I have waited for Thy salvation, Jehovah," through Samson the Danite, to the Messiah.[3]

1. *Samson's birth.* According to the chronological arrangement already indicated, we infer that Samson was born under the pontificate of Eli, and *after* the commencement of the Philistine oppression, which lasted forty years. If so, then his activity must have begun one or two years before the disastrous battle in which the ark fell into the hands of the Philistines, and in consequence of which Eli died (1 Sam. iv. 18).

While in the east and north the Ammonites oppressed Israel, the same sin had brought on the west and south of Palestine the judgment of Philistine domination. Then it was, that once more the Angel of Jehovah came, to teach the people, through Samson, that deliverance could only come by recalling and realising their Nazarite character as a priestly kingdom unto Jehovah; and that the Lord's Nazarite, so long as he remained such, would prove all-powerful through the strength of his God. The circumstances connected with the annunciation of Samson were supernatural. In the "secluded mountain village" of Zorah,[4] the modern *Surah*, about six hours west of Jerusalem, within the possession of Dan, lived *Manoah* ("resting") and his wife. Theirs, as we judge from the whole history, was the humble, earnest piety which, despite much apostacy, still lingered in Israel. It is to be observed that, like Sarah in the

---

distinguish between the ordinary Nazarite and the "Samson" or life-Nazarite. See my *Temple: its Ministry and Services at the time of Christ*, p. 328.

[1] Gen. xlix. 26.
[2] We have purposely adopted this rendering.
[3] Comp. Cassel, p. 122.
[4] Thomson, *The Land and the Book*, vol. ii. p. 361.

Old, and the mother of the Baptist in the New Testament, Manoah's wife was barren. For the child about to be born was not only to be God-devoted but God-given—and that in another sense even from his contemporary, Samuel, who had been God-asked of his mother. But in this case the Angel of the Covenant Himself came to announce the birth of a child, who should be "a Nazarite unto God from the womb," and who *as such* should "begin to deliver Israel out of the hand of the Philistines."[1] Accordingly, He laid on the mother, and still more fully on the unborn child, the Nazarite obligations as these are detailed in Numb. vi. 1–8, with the exception of that against defilement by contact with the dead, which evidently would have been incompatible with his future history.

The appearance of the Angel and His unnamedness had carried to the woman thoughts of the Divine, though she regarded the apparition as merely that of a man of God. Manoah had not been present; but in answer to his prayer a second apparition was vouchsafed. It added nothing to their previous knowledge, except the revelation of the real character of Him Who had spoken to them. For, when Manoah proposed to entertain his guest, he learned that He would not eat of his food, and that His name was "Wonderful." The latter, of course, in the sense of designating His character and working, for, as in the parallel passage, Is. ix. 6, such names refer not to the being and nature of the Messiah, but to His activity and manifestation—not to what He *is*, but to what He *does*. As suggested by the Angel, Manoah now brought a burnt-offering unto Jehovah—for, wherever He manifested Himself, there sacrifice and service might be offered. And when the Angel "did wondrously;" when fire leaped from the altar, and the Angel ascended in the flame that consumed the burnt-offering, then Manoah and his wife, recognising His nature, fell worshipping on the ground. No further revelation was granted

---

[1] The conjunction of the two in the text (Judges xiii. 5) indicates that they were to be regarded as cause and effect.

them; but when Manoah, in the spirit of the Old Testament, feared lest their vision of God might render it impossible for them to live on earth, his wife, more fully enlightened, strove to allay such doubts by the inference, that what God had begun in grace He would not end in judgment. An inference this, applying to all analogous cases in the spiritual history of God's people. And so months of patient, obedient waiting ensued, when at last the promised child was born, and obtained the name of Samson, or rather (in the Hebrew) *Shimshon*.[1] His calling soon appeared, for as the child grew up under the special blessing of the Lord, "the Spirit of Jehovah began to impel him in the camp of Dan, between Zorah and Eshtaol."[2]

2. About an hour south-west from Zorah, down[3] the rocky mountain-gorges, lay *Timnath*, within the tribal possession of Dan, but at the time held by the Philistines. This was the scene of Samson's first exploits. The "occasion" was his desire to wed a Philistine maiden. Against such union, as presumably contrary to the Divine will (Ex. xxxiv. 16; Deut. vii. 3), his parents remonstrated, not knowing "that it was of Jehovah, for he was seeking an occasion from (or on account of) the Philistines." Strictly speaking, the text only implies that this "seeking occasion on account of the Philistines" was directly from the Lord; his proposed marriage would be so only indirectly, as *affording* the desired occasion. Here then we again come upon man's individuality—his personal choice, as the motive power of which the Lord makes use for higher purposes. We leave aside the question, whether or not Samson had, *at the outset*, realised a higher Divine purpose in it all, and mark two points of vital importance in

---

[1] The name has been variously interpreted. By the Rabbis it is rendered "sunlike," in allusion to Ps. lxxxiv. 11. Others render it "mighty," "daring," or "he who lays waste."

[2] The exact locality cannot be ascertained. The Spirit of Jehovah began to *push*, to *drive*, or *impel* him.

[3] Hence the expression "Samson went down to Timnath." See Thomson.

this history. *First*, whenever Samson consciously subordinated his will and wishes to national and Divine purposes, he acted as a Nazarite, and "by faith;" whenever national and Divine purposes were made subservient to his own lusts, he failed and sinned. Thus we perceive throughout, side by side, *two elements* at work: the Divine and the human; Jehovah and Samson; the supernatural and the natural—intertwining, acting together, influencing each other, as we have so often noticed them throughout the course of Scripture history. *Secondly*, the influences of the Spirit of God upon Samson come upon him as *impulses* from without—sudden, mighty, and irresistible by himself and by others.

The misunderstanding and ignorance of Samson's motives on the part of his parents cannot fail to recall a similar opposition in the life of our Blessed Lord, even as, reverently speaking, this whole history foreshadows, though "afar off," that of our great Nazarite. But to return. Yielding at last to Samson, his parents, as the custom was, go with him to the betrothal at Timnath. All here and in the account of the marriage is strictly Eastern, and strictly Jewish. Nay, such is the tenacity of Eastern customs, that it might almost serve as descriptive of what would still take place in similar circumstances. But, under another aspect, we are here also on the track of direct Divine agency, all unknown probably to Samson himself. To this day "vineyards are very often far out from the villages, climbing up rough wádies and wild cliffs."[1] In one of these, precisely in the district where he would be likely to meet wild beasts, Samson encountered a young lion. "And the Spirit of Jehovah came mightily upon him," or "lighted upon him," the expression being notably the same as in 1 Sam. x. 10; xi. 6; xvi. 13; xviii. 10. Samson rent him, as he would have torn a kid.[2] This circumstance became "the occasion against the

---

[1] Thomson.
[2] Besides the parallel cases in Scripture (1 Sam. xvii. 34; 2 Sam. xxiii. 20), such writers as Winer and Cassel have collated many similar instances from well-accredited history.

Philistines." For, when soon afterwards Samson and his parents returned once more for the actual marriage, he found a swarm of bees in the dried skeleton of the lion. The honey,[1] which he took for himself and gave to his parents, became the occasion of a riddle which he propounded, after a custom usual in the East, to the "thirty companions" who acted as "friends of the bridegroom." The riddle proved too hard for them. Unwilling to bear the loss incurred by their failure—each "a tunic" and a "change-garment,"[2] these men threatened Samson's wife and her family with destruction. The woman's curiosity had from the first prompted her to seek the answer from her husband. But now her importunity, quickened by fear, prevailed. Of course, she immediately told the secret to her countrymen, and Samson found himself deceived and betrayed by his wife. But this was the "occasion" sought for. Once more "the Spirit of Jehovah lighted upon Samson." There was not peace between Israel and the Philistines, only an armed truce. And so Samson slew thirty men of them in Ashkelon, and with their spoil paid those who had answered his riddle. In his anger at her treachery he now forsook for a time his bride, when her father, as it were in contempt, immediately gave her to the first of the "bridegroom's friends."

This circumstance gave "occasion" for yet another deed. Samson returns again to his wife. Finding her the wife of another, he treats this as Philistine treachery against Israel, and declares to his father-in-law and to others around:[3] "This time I am blameless before the Philistines when I do evil unto them." The threatened "evil" consists in tying together, two and two, three hundred jackals, tail to tail, with a burning torch between them, and so sending the maddened animals

---

[1] Cassel notes the affinity between the Hebrew *devash*, honey, and the Saxon *wahs* or wax; and again between the Hebrew *doneg*, wax, and the Saxon *honec* or honey.

[2] These "change-garments" were costly raiment, frequently changed.

[3] Cassel thinks that the words were addressed by Samson to his Jewish countrymen; but this seems contrary to the whole context.

into the standing corn of the Philistines, which was just being harvested, into their vineyards, and among their olives. The destruction must have been terrible, and the infuriated Philistines took vengeance not upon Samson, but upon his wife and her family, by burning "her and her father with fire." This was cowardly as well as wicked, upon which Samson "said unto them, If (since) ye have done this, truly when I have been avenged upon you, and after that I will cease." The result was another great slaughter. But Samson, knowing the cowardice of his countrymen, felt himself now no longer safe among them, and retired to "the rock-cleft (rock-cave) *Etam*" ("the lair of wild beasts").

Samson's distrust had not been without sufficient ground. Afraid to meet Samson in direct conflict, the Philistines invaded the territory of Judah and spread in *Lehi*. Upon this, his own countrymen, as of old, not understanding "how that God by his hand would deliver them," actually came down to the number of 3000, to deliver Samson into the hand of the Philistines. Another parallel this, "afar off," to the history of Him whom His people delivered into the hands of the Gentiles! Samson offered no resistance, on condition that his own people should not attack him. Bound with two new cords, he was already within view of the hostile camp at Lehi; already he heard the jubilant shout of the Philistines, when once more "the Spirit of Jehovah came mightily upon him." Like flax at touch of fire, "flowed his bonds from off his hands."[1] This sudden turn of affairs, and manifestation of Samson's power, caused an immediate panic among the Philistines. Following up this effect, Samson seized the weapon readiest to hand, the jawbone of an ass, and with it slew company after company, "heap upon heap," till, probably in various encounters, no less than 1000 of the enemy strewed the ground. Only one more thing was requisite. All "this great deliverance" had evidently been given by Jehovah. But had Samson owned Him in it; had he fought and conquered "by faith," and as a

[1] So literally translated.

true Nazarite? Once more it is through the operation of natural causes, supernaturally overruled and directed, that Samson is now seen to have been the warrior of Jehovah, and Jehovah the God of the warrior. Exhausted by the long contest with the Philistines and the heat of the day, Samson sinks faint, and is ready to perish from thirst. Then God cleaves first, as it were, the rock of Samson's heart, so that the living waters of faith and prayer gush forth, before He cleaves the rock at Lehi. Such plea as his could not remain unheeded. Like that of Moses (Ex. xxxii. 31), or like the reasoning of Manoah's wife, it connected itself with the very covenant purposes of Jehovah and with His dealings in grace. After such battle and victory Samson could not have been allowed to perish from thirst; just as after our Lord's victory, He could not fail to see of the travail of His soul and be satisfied; and as it holds true of the Christian in his spiritual thirst, after the great conquest achieved for him: "He that spared not His own Son, but delivered Him up for us all, how shall He not with Him also freely give us all things?" (Rom. viii. 32.) Then, in answer to Samson's prayer, "God clave the hollow place which is in Lehi,"[1] probably a cleft in the rock, as erst He had done at Horeb (Ex. xvii. 6) and at Kadesh (Numb. xx. 8, 11). But the well which sprang thence, and of which, in his extremity, Samson had drunk, ever afterwards bore the significant name *En-hakkore*, the well of him that had called—nor had called in vain!

[1] This is *unquestionably* the meaning of the text, and not, as in the Authorised Version, "a hollow place that was in the jaw." The mistake has arisen from the circumstance that *Lehi* means a jaw-bone, the locality having obtained the name from Samson's victory with the jaw-bone (*Ramath-lehi*, "the hill or height of the jaw-bone," Judges xv. 17). The name *Lehi* is used *proleptically* in ver. 9, 14, that is, by anticipation.

CHAPTER XX

The Sin and Fall of Samson—Jehovah departs from him—Samson's Repentance, Faith, and Death.

(JUDGES XVI.)

THE closing verse of Judges xv. marks also the close of this period of Samson's life. Henceforth it is a record of the terrible consequences, first of using God's gift, intrusted for the highest and holiest purposes, for self-indulgence, and then of betraying and losing it. And this betrayal and loss are ever the consequence of taking for self what is meant for God, just as in the parable of the prodigal son the demand for the portion of goods which belonged to him is followed by the loss of all, by want and misery.

And here, in this its second stage, the history of Samson closely follows that of Israel. As Israel claimed for self, and would have used for self the gifts and calling of God; as it would have boasted in its Nazarite-strength and trusted in it, irrespective of its real meaning and the object of its bestowal, so now Samson. He goes down to Gaza, one of the fortified strongholds of the Philistines, *not* impelled by the Spirit of Jehovah, but for self-indulgence,[1] confident and boastful in what he regards as his own strength. Nor does that strength yet fail him, at least outwardly. For God is faithful to His promise, and so long as Samson has not cast away His help, it shall not fail him. But already he is on the road to it, and the night at Gaza must speedily be followed by the story of Delilah. Meanwhile, the men of Gaza and Samson must learn

---

[1] Cassel tries to prove that the place to which Samson went in Gaza was merely a hostelry—and so the ancient commentaries understood it But the language of the text does not bear out such interpretation.

another lesson—so far as they are capable of it. All night the guards are posted by the gates to wait for the dawn, when, as they expect, with the opening of the gates, Samson will leave the city, and they take him prisoner. During the night, however, they may take their sleep; for are not the gates strong and securely fastened? But, at midnight, Samson leaves the city, carrying with him its gates, and putting them down on "the top of a hill which faces towards Hebron,"[1] that is, at a distance of about half an hour to the south-east of Gaza.

Samson had once more escaped the Philistines; but the hour of his fall was at hand. To regard the God-intrusted strength as his own, and to abuse it for selfish purposes, was the first step towards betraying and renouncing that in which it really lay. Samson had ceased to be a Nazarite in heart before he ceased to be one outwardly. The story of Delilah[2] is too well known to require detailed repetition. Her very name—"the weak" or "longing one"—breathes sensuality, and her home is in the valley of Sorek, or of the choice red grape. The Philistine princes have learned it at last, that force cannot prevail against Samson, until by his own act of unfaithfulness he has deprived himself of his strength. It is the same story as that of Israel and its sin with Baal-Peor. The same device is adopted which Balaam had suggested for the ruin of Israel, and, alas! with the same success. The five princes of the Philistines promise each to give Delilah 1000 and 100 shekels, or 5500 in all, about £700, as the reward of her treachery. Three times has Samson eluded her persistency to find out his secret. Each time she has had watchers in an adjoining apartment ready to fall upon him, if he had really lost his strength. But the third time he had, in his trifling with sacred things, come dangerously near his fall, as in her hearing he

---

[1] So the text literally, and not, as in the Authorised Version, "the top of an hill that is before Hebron," for which, besides, the distance would have been far too great.

[2] The Rabbis have it, that if her name had not been Delilah, she would have obtained it, because she softened and weakened Samson's strength.

connected his strength with his hair. And yet, despite all warnings, like Israel of old, he persisted in his sin.

At last it has come. He has opened all his heart to Delilah, and she knows it. But Scripture puts the true explanation of the matter before us, in its usual emphatic manner, yet with such manifest avoidance of seeking for effect, that only the careful, devout reader will trace it. The facts are as follows: When Samson betrays his secret to Delilah, he says (xvi. 17): "If I be shaven, then my strength will go from me," whereas, when the event actually takes place, Scripture explains it: "He wot not that Jehovah was departed from him." In this contrast between his fond conceit about *his own* strength and the fact that it was due to *the presence of Jehovah*, lies the gist of the whole matter. As one writes: "The superhuman strength of Samson lay not in his uncut hair, but in this, that Jehovah was with him. But Jehovah was with him only so long as he kept his Nazarite vow." Or, in the words of an old German commentary: "The whole misery of Samson arose from this, that he appropriated to himself what God had done through him. God allows his strength to be destroyed, that in bitter experience he might learn, how without God's presence he was nothing at all. And so our falls always teach us best." But, as ever, sin proves the hardest taskmaster. Every indignity is heaped on fallen Samson. His eyes are put out; he is loaded with fetters of brass, and set to the lowest prison work of slaves. And here, also, the history of Samson finds its parallel in that of blinded Israel, with the judgment of bondage, degradation, and suffering, consequent upon their great national sin of casting aside their Nazarite vow.

But, blessed be God, neither the history nor its parallel stops here. For "the gifts and callings of God are without repentance." The sacred text expressly has it: "And the hair of his head began to grow, as it was shorn"—that is, *so soon* as it had been shorn. Then began a period of godly sorrow and repentance, evidenced both by the return of God to him, and by his last deed of faith, in which for his people he sacrificed his life; herein also following the great Antitype, though 'afar off." We imagine,[1] that "the lad," who led him to the pillars on which the house of Dagon rested was a Hebrew, cognisant of Samson's hopes and prayers, and who, immediately after having placed him in the fatal position, left the temple, and then carried the tidings to Samson's "brethren" (xvi. 31).

It is a high day in Gaza. From all their cities have the princes of the Philistines come up; from all the country around have the people gathered. The temple of the god *Dagon*—the fish-god, protector of the sea—is festively adorned and thronged. Below, the lords of the Philistines and all the chief men of the people are feasting at the sacrificial meal; above, along the roof, the gallery all around is crowded by three thousand men and women who look down on the spectacle beneath. It is a feast of thanksgiving to Dagon, of triumph to Philistia, of triumph against Jehovah and His people, and over captive Samson. The image of Dagon—the body of a fish with the head and hands of a man—which less than twenty years before had fallen and been broken before the ark of Jehovah (1 Sam. v. 4), stands once more proudly defying the God of Israel. And now the mirth and revelry have reached their highest point: Samson is brought in, and placed in the middle of the temple, between the central pillars which uphold the immense roof and the building itself. A few words whispered to his faithful Hebrew servant, and Samson's arms encircle the massive pillars. And then an unuttered agonising cry of repentance, of faith from the Nazarite, once more such, who will not only subordinate self to the nation and to his calling, but surrender life itself! Blind Samson is groping for a new light—and the brightness of another morning is already gilding his horizon. With all his might he bows himself. The pillars reel and give way. With one terrible crash fall roof and gallery, temple and image of Dagon; and in the ruins perish with Samson the lords of the Philistines and the flower of the people.

It has been told in Zorah. Gaza and Philistia are hushed

[1] The suggestion was first made by Cassel.

in awe and mourning. Samson's brethren and his father's house come down. From the ruins they search out the mangled body of the Nazarite. No one cares to interfere with them. Unmolested they bear away the remains, and lay them to rest in the burying-place of Manoah his father.

And so ends the period of the judges. Samson could have had no successor—he closed an epoch. But already at Shiloh a different reformation was preparing; and with different weapons will repentant Israel, under Samuel, fight against the Philistines, and conquer!

CHAPTER XXI.

Social and Religious Life in Bethlehem in the Days of the Judges—The Story of Ruth—King David's Ancestors.

(THE BOOK OF RUTH.)

YET another story of a very different kind from that of Samson remains to be told. It comes upon us with such sweet contrast, almost like a summer's morning after a night of wild tempest. And yet without this story our knowledge of that period would be incomplete.

It was "in the days when the judges judged"[1]—near the close of that eventful period. West of the Jordan, Jair and Eli held sway in Israel, while east of the river the advancing tide of Ammon had not yet been rolled back by Jephthah, the Gileadite. Whether the incursions of the Ammonites had carried want and wretchedness so far south into Judah as Bethlehem (Judges x. 9), or whether it was only due to strictly natural

---

[1] Critics differ widely as to the exact time when the events recorded in the Book of Ruth took place. Keil makes Boaz a contemporary of Gideon; but we have seen no reason to depart from the account of Josephus, who lays this history in the days of Eli.

causes, there was a "famine in the land," and this became, in the wonder-working Providence of God, one of the great links in the history of the kingdom of God.[1]

Bearing in mind the general characteristics of the period, and such terrible instances of religious apostacy and moral degeneracy as those recorded in the two Appendices to the Book of Judges (Judges xvii.–xxi.), we turn with a feeling of intense relief to the picture of Jewish life presented to us in the Book of Ruth.[2] Sheltered from scenes of strife and semi-heathenism, the little village of Bethlehem had retained among its inhabitants the purity of their ancestral faith and the simplicity of primitive manners. Here, embosomed amidst the hills of Judah, where afterwards David pastured his father's flocks, and where shepherds heard angels hail the birth of "David's greater Son," we seem to feel once again the healthful breath of Israel's spirit, and we see what moral life it was capable of fostering alike in the individual and in the family. If Boaz was, so to speak, the patriarch of a village, in which the old Biblical customs were continued, the humblest homes of Bethlehem must have preserved true Israelitish piety in its most attractive forms. For, unless the Moabitess Ruth had learned to know and love the land and the faith of Israel in the Bethlehemite household of Elimelech, transported as it was for a time into the land of Moab, she would not have followed so persistently her mother-in-law, away from her own home, to share her poverty, to work, if need be, even to beg, for her. And from such ancestry, nurtured under such circumstances, did the shepherd king of Israel spring, the ancestor and the type of the Lord and Saviour

---

[1] The Book of Ruth occupies an intermediate position between that of the Judges and those of Samuel—it is a supplement to the former and an introduction to the latter. So much "romance" has been thrown about the simple narrative of this book, as almost to lose sight of its real purport.

[2] The Book of Ruth numbers just eighty-five verses. In the Hebrew Bible it is placed among the *Hagiographa*, for dogmatic reasons on which it is needless to enter. In Hebrew MSS. it is among the five *Megilloth* "rolls" (Song, Ruth, Lamentations, Ecclesiastes, and Esther). Among the Jews it is very significantly read on the feast of weeks.

of men. These four things, then, seem the object of the Book of Ruth: to present a supplement by way of contrast to the Book of Judges; to show the true spirit of Israel; to exhibit once more the mysterious connection between Israel and the Gentiles, whereby the latter, at the most critical periods of Israel's history, seem most unexpectedly called in to take a leading part; and to trace the genealogy of David. Specially perhaps the latter two. For, as one has beautifully remarked:[1] If, as regards its contents, the Book of Ruth stands on the threshold of the history of David, yet, as regards its spirit, it stands, like the Psalms, at the threshold of the Gospel. Not merely on account of the genealogy of Christ, which leads up to David and Boaz, but on account of the spirit which the teaching of David breathes, do we love to remember that Israel's great king sprang from the union of Boaz and Ruth, which is symbolical of that between Israel and the Gentile world.

Everything about this story is of deepest interest—the famine in Bethlehem, "the house of bread," evidently caused, as afterwards its removal, by the visitation of God (Ruth i. 6); the hints about the family of Elimelech; even their names: Elimelech, "my God is king;" his wife, Naomi, "the pleasant," and their sons Mahlon (or rather Machlon) and Chilion (rendered by some "the weak," "the faint;" by others "the jubilant," "the crowned").[2] The family is described as "Ephrathites of Bethlehem-judah." The expression is apparently intended to convey, that the family had not been later immigrants, but original Jewish settlers—or, as the Jewish commentators have it, patrician burghers of the ancient Ephrath, or "fruitfulness" (Gen. xxxv. 19; xlviii. 7; comp. 1 Sam. xvii. 12; Micah v. 2). At one time the family seems to have been neither poor nor of inconsiderable standing (Ruth i. 19-21; ii.; iii.). But now, owing to "the

---

[1] Professor Cassel in his *Introduction to the Book of Ruth*.

[2] The rendering of the names by Josephus is evidently fanciful. The widely differing translations, which we have given in the text, show the divergence of critics, who derive the name from so very different roots.

famine," Ephrath was no onger "fruitfulness," nor yet Bethlehem "the house of bread;" and Elimelech, unable, on account of the troubles in the west, to go for relief either into Philistia or into Egypt, migrated beyond Jordan, and the reach of Israel's then enemies, to "sojourn" in Moab.

There is no need to attempt excuses for this separation from his brethren and their fate on the part of Elimelech, nor for his seeking rest among those hereditary enemies of Israel, outside Palestine, on whom a special curse seems laid (Deut. xxiii. 6). We have only to mark the progress of this story to read in it the judgment of God on this step. Of what befel the family in Moab, we know next to nothing. But this we are emphatically told, that Elimelech died a stranger in the strange land. Presently Machlon and Chilion married Moabite wives—Machlon, Ruth (Ruth iv. 10); Chilion, Orpah.[1] So other ten years passed. Then the two young men died, each childless, and Naomi was left desolate indeed. Thus, as one has remarked: "The father had feared not to be able to live at home. But scarcely had he arrived in the strange land when he died. Next, the sons sought to found a house in Moab; but their house became their grave. Probably, they had wished not to return to Judah, at least till the famine had ceased—and when it had ceased, they were no more. The father had gone away to have more, and to provide for his family—and his widow was now left without either children or possession!" Similarly, we do not feel it needful to attempt vindicating the marriage of these two Hebrew youths with Moabite wives. For there really was no express command against such unions. The instances in Scripture (Judges iii. 6; 1 Kings xi. 1; Neh. xiii. 23), which are sometimes quoted as proof to the contrary, are not in point, since they refer to the marriage of Hebrews *in the land of Israel*, not to that of those resident outside its boundaries (comp. Deut. vii. 3), and in the case of such marriages this is evidently an important element.

[1] Professor Cassel renders Ruth "the rose;" and Orpah "the hind." The *Midrash* makes Ruth a daughter of king Eglon.

And now tidings reached Moab, that "Jehovah had visited his people to give them bread." Naomi heard in it a call to return to her own land and home. According to eastern fashion, her daughters-in-law accompanied her on the way. When Naomi deemed that duty of proper respect sufficiently discharged, she stopped to dismiss them—as she delicately put it—to their "mother's" houses, with tenderly spoken prayer, that after all their sorrow the God of Israel would give them rest in a new relationship, as they had dealt lovingly both with the dead and with her. Closely examined, her words are found to convey, although with most exquisite delicacy, that, if her daughters-in-law went with her, they must expect to remain for ever homeless and strangers. She could offer them no prospect of wedded happiness in her own family, and she wished to convey to them, that no Israelite in his own land would ever wed a daughter of Moab. It was a noble act of self-denial on the part of the aged Hebrew widow by this plain speaking to strip herself of all remaining comfort, and to face the dark future, utterly childless, alone, and helpless. And when one of them, Orpah, turned back, though with bitter sorrow at the parting, Naomi had a yet more trying task before her. Ruth had, indeed, fully understood her mother-in-law's meaning; but there was another sacrifice which she must be prepared to make, if she followed Naomi. She must not only be parted from her people, and give up for ever all worldly prospects, but she must also be prepared to turn her back upon her ancestral religion. But Ruth had long made her choice, and the words in which she intimated it have deservedly become almost proverbial in the church. There is such ardour and earnestness about them, such resolution and calmness, as to lift them far above the sphere of mere natural affection or sense of duty. They intimate the deliberate choice of a heart which belongs in the first place to Jehovah, the God of Israel (i. 17), and which has learned to count all things but loss for the excellency of this knowledge. Although the story of Ruth has been invested with romance from its sequel, there is nothing romantic about her present resolve. Only the sternest prose of poverty is before her. Not to speak of the exceedingly depressing influence of her language (i. 13, 20, 21), Naomi had been careful to take from her any hope of a future, such as she had enjoyed in the past. In truth, the choice of Ruth is wholly unaccountable, except on the ground that she felt herself in heart and by conviction one of a Hebrew household—an Israelitish woman in soul and life, and that although she should in a sense be disowned by those with whom she had resolved to cast in her lot.

There was stir in the quiet little village of Bethlehem—especially among the women[1]—when Naomi unexpectedly returned after her long absence, and that in so altered circumstances. The lamentations of the widow herself made her even repudiate the old name of *Naomi* for *Mara* ("bitter"), for that "Jehovah" had "testified against," and "Shaddai"[2] afflicted her. Whether or not Naomi and her acquaintances really understood the true meaning of this "testifying" on the part of Jehovah, certain it is, that the temporary excitement of her arrival soon passed away, and the widow and her Moabite companion were left to struggle on alone in their poverty. Apparently no other near relatives of Elimelech were left, for Boaz himself is designated in the original as "an acquaintance to her husband,"[3] though the term indicates also relationship. And thus through the dreary winter matters only grew worse and worse, till at last early spring brought the barley-harvest.

It was one of those arrangements of the law, which, by its exquisite kindness and delicacy—in such striking contrast to the

---

[1] The Hebrew text significantly marks "they said," "call me not" (Ruth i. 20) with the *feminine* gender.

[2] Professor Cassel quotes parallel passages from Genesis to show that *Shaddai* means specially the God Who gives fruitfulness and increase.

[3] Not, as in the Authorised Version, "a kinsman of her husband's." The Rabbis make him a nephew of Elimelech, with as little reason as they represent Naomi and Ruth arriving just as they buried the first wife of Boaz! The derivation of the word *Boaz* is matter of dispute. We still prefer that which would render the name: "in him strength."

heathen customs of the time—shows its Divine origin, that what was dropped, or left, or forgotten in the harvest, was not to be claimed by the owner, but remained, as a matter of right, for the poor, the widows, and *emphatically* also for the " stranger." As if to confute the later thoughts of Jewish narrowness, " the stranger " alone is mentioned in *all* the three passages where this command occurs (Lev. xix. 9, 10 ; xxiii. 22 ; Deut. xxiv. 19–22).[1] Thus would the desolate share in Israel's blessings—and that as of Divine right rather than of human charity, while those who could no longer work for others might, as it were, work for themselves. Yet it must have been a bitter request, when Ruth, as if entreating a favour, asked Naomi's leave to go and glean in the fields, in the hope that she might " find favour " in the sight of master and reapers, so as not to be harshly spoken to, or roughly dealt with. And this was all —all that Ruth had apparently experienced of the " blessedness of following the Lord," for Whose sake she had left home and friends ! But there is a sublimeness in the words of Scripture which immediately follow—a carelessness of effect, and yet a startling surprise characteristic of God's dealings. As Ruth went on her bitter errand, not knowing whither, Scripture puts it :—" her hap happened the portion of field belonging to Boaz "—the same Divine " hap " by which sleep fled from Ahasuerus on that decisive night ; the same " hap " by which so often, what to the careless onlooker seems a chance " occurrence," is sent to us from God directly.

The whole scene is most vividly sketched. Ruth has come to the field of Boaz ; she has addressed herself to " the servant that was set over the reapers," and obtained his leave to " glean " after the reapers, and to " gather in the sheaves."[2] From early morn she has followed them, and, as the overseer afterwards

---

[1] May we ask those who doubt the early authorship of Deuteronomy, how they account for this circumstance?

[2] Professor Cassel has pointed out the distinction between the expression " in the sheaves " (ii. 7) and " between the sheaves " (ver. 15), the former being *after* the reapers, the latter *among* them.

informs Boaz (ii. 7), "her sitting in the house," whether for rest or talk, had been "but little."[1] And now the sun is high up in the heavens, when Boaz comes among his labourers. In true Israelitish manner he salutes them: "Jehovah with you!" to which they respond, "Jehovah bless thee!" He could not but have known "all the poor" (in the conventional sense) in Bethlehem, and Ruth must have led a very retired life, never seeking company or compassion, since Boaz requires to be informed who the Moabite damsel was. But though a stranger to her personally, the story of Ruth was well known to Boaz. Seen in the light of her then conduct and bearing, its spiritual meaning and her motives would at once become luminous to Boaz. For such a man to know, was to do what God willed. Ruth was an Israelite indeed, brave, true, and noble. She must not go to any other field than his; she must not be treated like ordinary gleaners, but remain *there*, where he had spoken to her, "by the maidens," so that, as the reapers went forwards, and the maidens after them to bind the sheaves, she might be the first to glean; she must share the privileges of his household; and he must take care that she should be unmolested.

It is easier, even for the children of God, to bear adversity than prosperity, especially if it come after long delay and unexpectedly. But Ruth was "simple" in heart; or, as the New Testament expresses it, her "eye was single," and God preserved her. And now, in the altered circumstances, she still acts quite in character with her past. She complains not of her poverty; she explains not how unused she had been to such circumstances; but she takes humbly, and with surprised gratitude, that to which she had no claim, and which as a "stranger" she had not dared to expect. Did she, all the while, long for a gleam of heaven's light—for an Israelitish welcome, to tell her that all this came from the God of Israel, and for His sake? It was granted her, and that more fully

---

[1] So correctly, and not as in the Authorised Version, which misses the meaning.

than she could have hoped. Boaz knew what she had done for man, and what she had given up for God. Hers, as he now assured her, would be recompense for the one, and a *full* reward of the other, and that from Jehovah, the God of Israel, under Whose wings she had come to trust. And now for the first time, and when it is past, the secret of her long-hidden sorrow bursts from Ruth, as she tells it to Boaz: "Thou hast consoled me, and spoken to the heart of thine handmaid."

What follows seems almost the natural course of events—natural, that Boaz should accord to her the privileges of a kinswoman; natural also, that she should receive them almost unconscious of any distinction bestowed on her—keep and bring home part even of her meal to her mother-in-law (ii. 18), and still work on in the field till late in the evening (ver. 17). But Naomi saw and wondered at what Ruth's simplicity and modesty could have never perceived. Astonished at such a return of a day's gleaning, she had asked for details, and then, without even waiting to hear her daughter's reply, had invoked God's blessing on the yet unknown dispenser of this kindness. And so Ruth the Moabitess has begun to teach the language of thanksgiving to her formerly desponding Hebrew mother! But when she has told her story, as before to Boaz, so now to Naomi its spiritual meaning becomes luminous. In her weakness, Naomi had murmured; in her unbelief, she had complained; she had deemed herself forsaken of God and afflicted. All the while, however she and hers might have erred and strayed, God had never left off His kindness either to the living or to the dead![1] And it is only after she has thus given thanks, that she explains to the astonished Ruth: "The man is near unto us—he *is one* of our redeemers" (comp. Lev. xxv. 25; Deut. xxv. 5). Still even so, no further definite thoughts seem to have shaped themselves in the mind of either of the women. And so Ruth continued in quiet work

---

[1] It has been rightly observed, that this acknowledgment implied belief in the immortality of the soul—that the dead had not perished, but only gone from hence.

in the fields of Boaz all the barley-harvest and unto the end of the wheat-harvest, a period of certainly not less than two months.

But further thought and observation brought a new resolve to Naomi. The two months which had passed had given abundant evidence of the utter absence of all self-consciousness on the part of Ruth, of her delicacy and modesty in circumstances of no small difficulty. If these rare qualities must have been observed by Naomi, they could not have remained unnoticed by Boaz, as he daily watched her bearing. Nor yet could Ruth have been insensible to the worth, the piety, and the kindness of him who had been the first in Israel to speak comfort to her heart. That, in such circumstances, Naomi, recognising a true Israelitess in her daughter-in-law, should have sought "rest" for her—and that rest in the house of Boaz, was alike to follow the clear indications of Providence, and what might be called the natural course of events. Thus, then, all the actors in what was to follow were prepared to take their parts. The manner in which it was brought about must not be judged by our western notions, although we are prepared to defend its purity and delicacy in every particular. Nor could Naomi have well done otherwise than counsel as she did. For the law which fixed on the next-of-kin the duty of redeeming a piece of land (Lev. xxv. 25), did *not* connect with it the obligation of marrying the childless widow of the owner, which (strictly speaking) only devolved upon a brother-in-law (Deut. xxv. 5); although such seems to have been the law of custom in Bethlehem, and this, as we believe, in strict accordance with the *spirit* and object, if not with the *letter* of the Divine commandment. Thus Naomi had no *legal* claim upon Boaz—not to speak of the fact, of which she must have been aware, that there was a nearer kinsman than he of Elimelech in Bethlehem. Lastly, in accordance with the law, it was not Naomi but Ruth who must lay claim to such marriage (Deut. xxv. 7, 8).

Yet we should miss the whole spirit of the narrative, if, while admitting the influence of other matters, we were not to recognise that the law of redemption and of marriage with a childless widow, for the purpose of "not putting out a name in Israel," had been the guiding principle in the conduct of all these three—Naomi, Ruth, and Boaz. And, indeed, of the value and importance of this law there cannot be fuller proof than that furnished by this story itself—bearing in mind that from this next-of-kin-union descended David, and, "according to the flesh," the Lord Jesus Christ, the Son of David.

Keeping all this in view, we proceed to gather up the threads of our story. By the advice of her mother-in-law, Ruth puts off alike her widow's and her working dress. Festively arrayed as a bride—though, assuredly, not to be admired by Boaz, since the transaction was to take place at *night*—she goes to the threshing-floor, where, as the wind sprang up at even, Boaz was to winnow his barley. Unobserved, she watcheth where he lies down, and, softly lifting the coverlet, lays herself at his feet. At midnight, accidentally touching the form at his feet, Boaz wakes with a start—and "bent down, and, behold a woman lying at his feet!" In reply to his inquiry, the few words she speaks—exquisitely beautiful in their womanly and Scriptural simplicity—explain her conduct and her motive. Two things here require to be kept in mind: Boaz himself sees nothing strange or unbecoming in what Ruth has done; on the contrary, he praises her conduct as surpassing all her previous claims to his respect. Again, the language of Boaz implies that Ruth, although daring what she had felt to be right, had done it with the fear which, in the circumstances, womanly modesty would prompt. We almost seem to hear the low whispered tones, and the tremor of her voice, as we catch the gentle, encouraging words of Boaz' reply: "My daughter," and as he stills the throbbing of her heart with his kindly-spoken, fatherly: "Fear not!" No thought but of purity and goodness,[1] and of Israel's law intruded on

---

[1] Professor Cassel reminds us of a legal determination in the *Mishnah* (*Yebam.* ii. 8), which the learned reader may compare. The reference,

the midnight converse of those who were honoured to become the ancestors of our Lord.

And now he, on his part, has explained to Ruth, how there is yet a nearer kinsman, whose claims must first be set aside, if the law is to be strictly observed. And, assuredly, if observance of the law of redemption, with all that it implied in Israel, had not been the chief actuating motive of Boaz and Ruth, there would have been no need first to refer the matter to the nearer kinsman, since there could be no possible hindrance to the union of those whose hearts evidently belonged to each other.

The conduct of each party having been clearly determined, they lie down again in silence. What remained of the short summer's night soon passed. Before the dawn had so far brightened that one person could have recognised another, she left the threshing-floor, bearing to her mother the gift of her kinsman, as if in pledge that her thoughts had been understood by him, and that her hope concerning the dead and the living would be realised.[1]

The story now hastens to a rapid close. Early in the morning Boaz goes up to the gate, the usual place for administering law, or doing business. He sits down as one party to a case; calls the unnamed nearer kinsman, as he passes by, to occupy the place of the other party, and ten of the elders as witnesses or umpires—the number *ten* being not only symbolical of completeness, but from immemorial custom, and afterwards by law, that which constituted a legal assembly. To understand what passed between Boaz and the unnamed kinsman, we must offer certain explanations of the

---

though apt, however, rather breaks in as prose upon the sublime beauty of the scene. It needed not such determinations to guard the purity of the threshing-floor of Boaz.

[1] We mention, without pronouncing any opinion upon it, that some—alike Jews and Christians—have seen a symbolism in the number *six* of the measures of barley which Ruth brought with her, as if days of work and toil were done, and "rest" about to be granted.

state of the case and of the law applying to it, different from any hitherto proposed. For the difficulty lies in the sale of the property by Naomi—nor is it diminished by supposing that she had not actually disposed of, but was only offering it for sale. In general we may here say, that the law (Numb. xxvii. 8, 11) does *not* deal with any case precisely similar to that under consideration. It only contemplates one of two things, the death of a childless man, when his next-of-kin (speaking broadly) *is bound* to marry his widow (Deut. xxv. 5); or else a forced sale of property through poverty, when the next-of-kin of the original proprietor may redeem the land (Lev. xxv. 25). It is evident, that the former must be regarded as a *duty*, the latter as a *privilege* attaching to kinship, the object of both being precisely the same, the preservation of the family (rather than of the individual) in its original state. But although the law does not mention them, the same principle would, of course, apply to all analogous cases. Thus it might, for example, be, that a man would marry the widow, but be unable to redeem the property. On the other hand, he never could claim to redeem property without marrying the widow, to whom as the representative of her dead husband the property attached. In any case the property of the deceased husband was vested in a childless widow. In fact, so long as the childless widow lived, no one could have any claim on the property, since she was potentially the heir of her deceased husband. All authorities admit, that in such a case she had the use of the property, and a passage in the Mishnah (*Yebam.* iv. 3) declares it lawful for her to sell possessions, though it does seem very doubtful whether the expression covers the sale of her deceased husband's *land*. Such, however, would have been in strict accordance with the principle and the spirit of the law. In the case before us then, the property still belonged to Naomi, though in reversion to Ruth as potentially representing Elimelech and Machlon, while the claim to be married to the next-of-kin could, of course, in the circumstances, only devolve upon Ruth. Thus the property still held by Naomi went, in equity and in law, with the hand of Ruth, nor had any one claim upon the one without also taking the other. No kinsman had performed the kinsman's *duty* to Ruth, and therefore no kinsman could claim the *privilege* of redemption connected with the land. With the hand of Ruth the land had, so to speak, been repudiated. But as the kinsman had virtually refused to do his part, and Naomi was unable to maintain her property, she disposed of it, and that quite in the spirit of the law. There was no wrong done to any one. The only ground for passing the land to a kinsman would have been, that he would preserve the name of the dead. But this he had virtually refused to do. On the other hand, it was still open to him to redeem the land, if, at the same time, he would consent to wed Ruth. It would have been the grossest injustice to have allowed the privilege of redeeming a property to the kinsman who refused to act as kinsman. Instead of preserving a name in Israel, it would in reality have extinguished it for ever.

This was precisely the point in discussion between Boaz and the unnamed kinsman. Boaz brought, first, before him the *privilege* of the kinsman: redemption of the land. This he accepted. But when Boaz next reminded him, that this privilege carried with it a certain *duty* towards Ruth, and that, if the latter were refused, the former also was forfeited, he ceded his rights to Boaz.[1] The bargain was ratified according to ancient custom in Israel by a symbolical act, of which we find a modification in Deut. xxv. 9. Among all ancient nations the "shoe" was a symbol either of departure (Ex. xii. 11), or of taking possession (comp. Psalm x. 8).[2] In this instance

---

[1] The reason which he assigns (Ruth iv. 6), admits of different interpretations. Upon the whole I still prefer the old view, that his son by Ruth would have been the sole heir—the more so, that in this particular case (as we find in the sequel, iv. 15) Ruth's son would be obliged to be "the nourisher" of Naomi's "old age."

[2] A popular illustration of the former is the custom of throwing a shoe after a bride on her departure from her father's home. This also explains the custom of kissing the Pope's slipper, as claiming possession of, and dominion in the Church.

the kinsman handed his shoe to Boaz—that is, ceded his possession to him. Alike the assembled elders, and those who had gathered around to witness the transaction, cordially hailed its conclusion by wishes which proved, that "all the city knew that Ruth was a virtuous woman," and were prepared to receive the Moabitess as a mother in Israel, even as Thamar had proved in the ancestry of Boaz.

It had all been done in God and with God, and the blessing invoked was not withheld. A son gladdened the hearts of the family of Bethlehem. Naomi had now a "redeemer," not only to support and nourish her, nor merely to "redeem" the family property, but to preserve the name of the family in Israel. And that "redeemer"—a child, and yet not a child of Boaz; a redeemer-son, and yet not a son of Naomi—was the father of Jesse. And so the story which began in poverty, famine, and exile leads up to the throne of David. Undoubtedly this was the main object for which it was recorded: to give us the history of David's family; and with his genealogy, traced not in every link but in symbolical outline,[1] the Book of Ruth appropriately closes. It is the only instance in which a book is devoted to the domestic history of a woman, and that woman a stranger in Israel. But that woman was the Mary of the Old Testament.

[1] This is not the place to enter into the question of the Old Testament genealogies, but it is evident that five names cannot cover the period of 430 years in Egypt, nor yet other five that from the Exodus to David. On the other hand, it deserves notice that the names mentioned amount exactly to ten—the number of perfection, and that these are again arranged into twice five, each division covering very nearly the same length of period.

THE END.

www.ingramcontent.com/pod-product-compliance
Lightning Source LLC
Chambersburg PA
CBHW032137160426
43197CB00008B/674